ACT®
All-Nighter

SPARKNOTES

SparkNotes would like to thank Ben Paris for his contributions to this book and
Eric Goodman for his role as series editor.

Interior icon © Matt Wiegle

Spark Publishing
A Division of Barnes & Noble
120 Fifth Avenue
New York, NY 10011

Library of Congress Cataloging-in-Publication Data

ACT All-Nighter.
    p. cm.
  ISBN-13: 978-1-4114-0522-6 (pbk.)
  ISBN-10: 1-4114-0522-6 (pbk.)
  1. ACT Assessment—Study guides.

LB2353.48.A265 2008
378.1'662—dc22

                                          2008001471

Printed and bound in the United States

10 9 8 7 6 5 4 3 2 1

Contents

Introduction

HAVE YOU EVER HAD A DREAM IN WHICH YOU'RE ABOUT TO take a crucial final exam and realize you haven't attended a single class all semester? Or that you're about to make a major presentation in front of hundreds of people only to realize you're standing there in your underwear? Well, we can't help you with that last one . . . but if that first dream is coming true—your ACT is fast approaching and you've barely begun to prepare—then you've come to the right place.

SparkNotes' *ACT All-Nighter* is intended to provide you with the largest leap in ACT proficiency in the shortest amount of time. If your test is a week away, or even if it's just one or two nights before the test and you need a last-minute crash course, this book provides a number of key strategies and techniques that will help you on test day.

Before we begin, we urge you to adopt a positive mindset for the task ahead. Why you're in your present predicament is of no concern. Maybe you've been busy at school, at work, or with family responsibilities. Maybe your dog ate your ACT homework. Who knows, and *who cares*? The point is that you still have some time before your test, and you need to make the most of it. You may feel that you're already behind the eight ball, but the point of this book is to show you that definite improvement is possible in the short term if you put in some effort each day to learn and absorb the information we present.

HOW TO USE THIS BOOK

Following this section, you'll encounter our ACT mini-test. This will give you a quick taste of the types of questions you can expect to encounter on the

ACT. More important, you can easily get a rough sense of your strengths and weaknesses and focus your study time accordingly.

The heart of this book consists of four "Intensives"—chapters that *intensely* distill the most important elements of the ACT. These Intensives cover the fundamentals—what you absolutely need to know for test day.

We've designed the Intensives so that you can work through each one in a few hours. Each Intensive has expert strategies, step methods, techniques, and practice questions to give you the opportunity to apply what you've learned. If you have time to work through the whole book, by all means do so. But if you don't, use the mini-test to help you decide which parts of the book might be most valuable *for you* at this stage of the game. We conclude with the Top 15 Test-Day Tips, designed to help you put your best test-taking foot forward on the big day.

ACT BASICS

The ACT is a little less than three hours long. It's divided into four Subject Tests: English, Math, Reading, and Science. There's also an optional Writing Test, which, if taken, will increase your total testing time by thirty minutes. Read on for more info . . .

Structure

The four required ACT Subject Tests and optional Writing Test always appear in the following order:

SUBJECT TEST	NUMBER OF QUESTIONS	TIME
English	75	45 minutes
Math	60	60 minutes
Reading	40	35 minutes
Science	40	35 minutes
Writing	n/a	30 minutes

On test day, you'll likely get a short break between the Math and Reading Tests and before the Writing Test—if you're taking it, that is. You don't *have* to take the Writing Test, so it probably isn't a huge priority for you at this point, which is why we don't cover it in this book. We cover the four required tests in Intensives 1–4.

Scoring

For every question you answer correctly, you receive one point. There's no penalty for wrong answers. The total number of questions you answer correctly is called your *raw score*. You'll receive four raw scores, one for each Subject Test. You'll also receive several raw subscores for each section of the Subject Test (for example, Usage/Mechanics and Rhetorical Skills are the two subsections of the English Test). If you take the Writing Test, your raw scores on the English and Writing Tests will be combined into one score. Based on the raw scores of every test taker who took a particular ACT, the test makers work out a mathematical curve, feed your raw score into a computer, and get what's known as your *scaled score*, a number between 1 and 36, for each of your four raw scores.

Your four scaled scores are then averaged, producing the *composite score*. That's the biggie, the one colleges really care about. The composite score is an average, so each of the four Subject Tests count equally. Finally, every composite score is assigned a corresponding *percentile ranking*, indicating how you fared in comparison to other test takers. A perfect ACT composite score is 36.

Registering for the Test

The fastest way to register for the ACT is to sign up at **www.actstudent.org**. You can also register by mail, using an ACT registration packet, available at your school counselor's office. The fee changes depending on whether you're taking the optional Writing Test.

When to Take the ACT

The ACT is offered several times a year, usually in February, April, June, October, and December. Most students take the ACT for the first time in the spring of their junior years—that means either in April or June. Depending on their scores, many students then decide to take the test again in the fall of their senior years. If you're planning to take the test a second time, make sure you take it early enough so that your score will reach colleges before the application deadline passes. Bottom line: Check with the schools to which you are applying and make sure that you're on track to take the test by the correct date.

GENERAL ACT STRATEGIES

We'll spend the rest of this introduction discussing a few general ACT pointers to keep in mind before you immerse yourself in the mini-test and Intensives. These strategies apply to every ACT Subject Test. We list them here because you should always have them in the back of your mind as you study and as you take the ACT:

- Set a Target Score
- Memorize the Instructions
- Use the Booklet As Scratch Paper
- Answer Easy Questions First
- Guess Intelligently
- Don't Be Afraid to Bail
- Avoid Carelessness
- Mine the Experience

You don't need to focus on the general strategies obsessively, but you should be sure not to forget them. They will help you save time and cut down on careless errors.

Set a Target Score

Before you begin studying for the ACT, you need to set a realistic scoring goal. This is a good strategy for any test taker but applies even more to those working within a short preparation time frame. To set a target score, take a look at the average ACT scores at the colleges to which you're applying. You should try to get a score that's a few points higher than the average at your first-choice school.

If you're gunning for a perfect score, you'll need to answer just about every question correctly. But if you're looking to score something a little less ambitious, you can skip or guess on questions that are really long or on question types that give you trouble.

Memorize the Instructions

You'll need all the time you can get, so don't waste time reading the test instructions during the actual test. Each Intensive begins with an X-ray in which we discuss the directions for each test. Memorize them now so that you can skip them on test day.

Use the Booklet As Scratch Paper

You should write down your work for all math problems, in case you want to return to them later to complete questions or check your answers. But you should also make notes alongside the Reading and Science passages; doing so will help you stay on track when answering the subsequent questions. In addition, if you want to skip a question and come back to it later, you should make a distinctive mark next to it so that you won't miss it on your second pass through the questions.

Answer Easy Questions First

All questions are worth the same number of points, so there's no reason to slave away over a difficult question if doing so requires several minutes. In the same amount of time, you probably could have racked up points by answering a bunch of easy, less time-consuming questions. Answer the easy and moderate questions first (the ACT lets you skip around within a test). That way you'll make sure you get to see all the questions on the test that you have a good shot of getting right, while saving the leftover time for the difficult questions.

Remember, though, that which questions are easy or moderate and which are difficult is largely up to you. Generally speaking, questions on the Math Test are ordered by level of difficulty, with easier questions coming first and harder questions coming later in the section. Science Test questions are also largely ordered by difficulty, with the harder passages coming later. In reality, though, it doesn't matter how the test makers order the questions—whether by difficulty or by content tested. What matters is how easy or hard *you* find the questions. As you work through each test, trust your instincts: If you think a question is easy, it probably is. Figure out the answer and move on to the next one. If you think a question is hard, flag it and come back to it, once you've answered the easier questions.

Guess Intelligently

Whenever you can't answer a question on the ACT, you must guess. Don't leave any questions blank. You aren't penalized for getting a question wrong, so guessing can only help your score. Don't ever forget that the ACT is a multiple-choice test, which means the correct answers are always right there in front of you. Of course, the test makers don't just give you the correct answer; they hide it among a bunch of incorrect answer choices. Your job on each question is to find the right answer. Eliminating answer choices and making an educated guess on tough questions increases the likelihood that you'll get the question correct.

There are actually two kinds of guesses: random and intelligent. Random guesser Charlie Franklin will always guess **C** (on odd-numbered questions) or **F** (on even-numbered questions) because he really, really likes those letters. Using this method, Charlie has a pretty good chance of getting about 25 percent of the questions right, yielding a composite score of about 11. That's not too shabby, considering Charlie expended practically no intellectual energy beyond identifying **C** and **F** as the first letters of his first and last name.

In contrast, intelligent guesser Celia works to eliminate answers, always getting rid of two choices for each question. She then guesses between the remaining choices and has a 50 percent chance of getting the correct answer. Celia will therefore get about half of the questions on the test correct. Her composite score will be about a 19, which is an average score on the ACT. The example of these two guessers should show you that while random guessing can help you, educated guessing can really help you. "Always guess" really means "always eliminate as many answer choices as possible and then guess"—that's guessing intelligently.

Don't Be Afraid to Bail

If you've spent a significant amount of time on a problem and haven't gotten close to answering it, let it go. Leaving a question unfinished may seem like giving up or wasting time you've already spent, but you can come back to the problem after you've answered the easy ones. The time you spent on the problem earlier won't be wasted. When you come back to the problem, you'll already have done part of the work needed to solve it.

Avoid Carelessness

It's easy to make mistakes if you're moving too quickly through the questions. Speeding through the test can result in misinterpreting a question or missing a crucial piece of information. You should always be aware of this kind of error because the test makers have written the test with speedy test takers in mind: Test makers often include tempting "partial answers" among the answer choices. A partial answer is the result of some, but not all, of the steps needed to solve a problem. If you rush through a question, you may mistake a partial answer for the real answer.

You should also be careful when bubbling in your answers. An easy way to prevent slips on the ACT answer sheet is to pay attention to the letters being bubbled. Odd-numbered answers are lettered **A**, **B**, **C**, **D** (except on the Math Test, where they are **A**, **B**, **C**, **D**, **E**), and even-numbered answers are lettered **F**, **G**, **H**, **J** (except on the Math Test, where they are **F**, **G**, **H**, **J**, **K**).

You may also want to try bubbling in groups (five at a time or a page at a time) rather than answering one by one. Circle the answers in the test booklet as you go through the page, and then transfer the answers over to the answer sheet as a group. This method should increase your speed and accuracy in filling out the answer sheet. To further increase your accuracy, say the question number and the answer in your head as you fill out the grid: "Number 24, **F**. Number 25, **C**. Number 26, **J**."

Mine the Experience

You'll want to review every practice question in order to reinforce what each one teaches for test day. "Well, duh," you're probably thinking. "Of course I'm going to see if I got it right and check what I did wrong if I didn't." But you've got to go beyond that: Did you get it right for the right reason? Did you just get lucky, or is the process you used repeatable in the future? If you got it wrong, was your mistake simply careless, or does it indicate a lack of understanding regarding a particular concept? Each question offers a wealth of information, and the more you get out of each one, the fewer questions you'll need to do to bump up your score in the time remaining before the test. We therefore implore to you "mine the experience" of every exercise and example we present in this book.

On to the ACT mini-test!

ACT Mini-Test

THE FOLLOWING MINI-TEST INCLUDES EXAMPLES OF THE types of questions found in each of the scored sections of the ACT. An answer key follows. See how you make out on each part, and then decide which Intensives warrant the most attention. If you have the time, work fully through all the Intensives. If you don't, use your performance on this mini-test to budget your time accordingly.

THE ENGLISH TEST

DIRECTIONS: There are two question formats within the passages. In one format, you will find words and phrases that have been underlined and assigned numbers. These numbers will correspond with sets of alternative words/phrases. From the sets of alternatives, choose the answer choice that works best in context, keeping in mind whether it employs standard written English, whether it gets across the idea of the section, and whether it suits the tone and style of the passage. You will usually be offered the option "NO CHANGE," which you should choose if you think the version found in the passage is best.

In the second format, you will see boxed numbers referring to sections of the passage or to the passage as a whole. In the right-hand column, you will be asked questions about or given alternatives for the sections marked by the boxes. Choose the answer choice that best answers the question or completes the section.

[1] That summer my parents <u>buy</u>
        1
me my first bike—my first true love.

[2] One day, I crashed into a tree and

broke my leg. [3] Unfortunately, my

control of the bike was not as great as

my enthusiasm for it. [4] I spent all

my afternoons speeding around the

neighborhood blocks. [2]

1.   **A.** NO CHANGE
     B. bought
     C. have bought
     D. buys

2.   Which of the following provides the most logical ordering of the sentences in the paragraph?
     F. 3, 2, 1, 4
     G. 3, 1, 4, 2
     H. 1, 4, 3, 2
     J. 1, 4, 2, 3

An audience of thousands of expectant

people who have come from afar to listen

to live music in an outdoor setting <u>seem</u>
                                        3
terrifying to a nervous performer.

3.   **A.** NO CHANGE
     B. seems
     C. have seemed
     D. to seem

<u>Me and Jesse</u> went to Cosmic Bowling
     4
Night at the Bowladrome.

4.   **F.** NO CHANGE
     G. Jesse and me
     H. Jesse and I
     J. I and Jesse

[2]

Victorian novelists were often concerned with issues of character, plot, and the Victorian social world. Dickens's novels, for example, were several-hundred-page-long works documenting the elaborate inter-weaving of his characters.

[3]

[5] Their "modernist" novels to tended focus on the characters' inner lives, which they depicted through a stylistic technique called "stream of consciousness." Several of the best-known modernist novels were written in this stream-of-consciousness style.

5. The writer wishes to begin Paragraph 3 with a sentence that strengthens the focus of the paragraph, while providing a transition from Paragraph 2. Which of the following would be the best choice?

A. In the early twentieth century, novelists began to reject the Victorian emphasis on social context and look for a new focus for the novel.

B. Victorian novels ended with the Victorian era.

C. In the early twentieth century, novelists further developed this emphasis on characters' inner lives.

D. World War I significantly affected British culture in the twentieth century.

THE MATH TEST

ACT All-Nighter

DIRECTIONS: After solving each problem, pick the correct answer from the five given. Calculators can be used for any problem on the test, though calculators may be more harm than help for some questions.

Note: Unless otherwise stated on the test, you should assume the following:

1. Figures accompanying questions are not drawn to scale.
2. Geometric figures exist in a plane.
3. When given in a question, "line" refers to a straight line.
4. When given in a question, "average" refers to the arithmetic mean.

1. If $\dfrac{x+28}{7} = 8$, then what is the value of x?

   A. 84
   B. 56
   C. 52
   D. 28
   E. 2

2. A classroom contains 31 chairs, some of which have arms and some of which do not. If the room contains 5 more armchairs than chairs without arms, how many armchairs does it contain?

   F. 10
   G. 13
   H. 16
   J. 18
   K. 21

14

3. What is the value of x if $3x - 27 = 33$?

A. 2
B. 11
C. 20
D. 27
E. 35

[handwritten: $3x - 27 = 33$ $+27 +27$ $3x = \frac{60}{3} = 20$]

4. At a local golf club, 75 members attend weekday lessons, 12 members attend weekend lessons, and 4 members attend both weekday and weekend lessons. If 10 members of the organization do not attend any lessons, how many members are in the club?

[handwritten: $75 + 12 + 10 + 4$]

F. 65
G. 75
H. 82
J. 93
K. 101

5. If the average of 13, 6, 9, x, and y is 12, what is the average of $x + y$?

A. 6
B. 9
C. 12
D. 16
E. 32

[handwritten: $\frac{13 + 6 + 9 + x + y}{5} = 12$]

[handwritten: $13 + 6 + 9$ $28 + x + y = 60$ -28 32]

THE READING TEST

DIRECTIONS: Read the passage, then answer the questions that follow.

SOCIAL SCIENCE: This passage is adapted from Doris Stevens's *Jailed for Freedom* (1920).

"Where are the people?" This was Woodrow Wilson's first question as he arrived at the Union Station in Washington the day before his first inauguration to the Presidency in March, 1913.

"On the Avenue watching the suffragists parade," came the answer.

5 The suffrage issue was brought to his attention from then on until his final surrender. It lay entirely with him as to how long women would be obliged to remind him of this issue before he decided to take a hand.

"The people" were on the Avenue watching the suffragists parade. The informant was quite right. It seemed to those of us who attempted to march
10 for our idea that day that the whole world was there—packed closely on Pennsylvania Avenue.

The purpose of the procession was to dramatize in numbers the fact that women wanted to vote. What politicians had not been able to get through their minds we would give them through their eyes—often a powerful substitute. Our
15 first task seemed simple: to show that thousands of women wanted immediate action on their long delayed enfranchisement. This we did.

The Administration, without intending it, played into the hands of the women from this moment. The women had been given a permit to march. Inadequate police protection allowed roughs to attack them and all but break up the pageant.
20 The fact of ten thousand women marching with banners and bands for this idea was startling enough to wake up the government and the country, but not so startling as ten thousand women manhandled by irresponsible crowds because of police indifference.

An investigation was demanded and a perfunctory one held. The police
25 administration was exonerated, but when the storm of protest had subsided the Chief of Police was quietly retired to private life.

A few days later the first deputation of suffragists ever to appear before a President in order to enlist his support waited upon President Wilson. Alice Paul led the deputation. The President received the deputation in the White House
30 Offices. When the women entered they found five chairs arranged in a row with one chair in front, like a classroom. All confessed to being frightened when the

President came in and took his seat at the head of the class. The President said he had no opinion on the subject of woman suffrage; that he had never given it any thought; and that above all it was his task to see that Congress concentrated
35 on the currency revision and the tariff reform. It is recorded that the President was somewhat taken aback when Miss Paul addressed him during the course of the interview with this query, "But Mr. President, do you not understand that the Administration has no right to legislate for currency, tariff, and any other reform without first getting the consent of women to these reforms?"
40 "Get the consent of women?" It was evident that this course had not heretofore occurred to him.

"This subject will receive my most careful consideration," was President Wilson's first suffrage promise.

He was given time to "consider" and a second deputation went to him, and still
45 a third, asking him to include the suffrage amendment in his message to the new Congress assembling the following month.

He flatly said there would be no time to consider suffrage for women. But the "unreasonable" women kept right on insisting that the liberty of half the American people was paramount to tariff and currency. President Wilson's
50 first session of Congress came together April 7th, 1913. The opening day was marked by the suffragists' second mass demonstration. This time women delegates representing every one of the 435 Congressional Districts in the country bore petitions from the constituencies showing that the people "back home" wanted the amendment passed. The delegates marched on Congress.
55 The same day the amendment which bears the name of Susan B. Anthony, who drafted it in 1875, was reintroduced into both houses of Congress.

The month of May saw monster demonstrations throughout the country, with the direct result that in June the Senate Committee on Suffrage made the first favorable report made by that committee in twenty-one years, thereby placing it
60 on the Senate calendar for action.

Not relaxing the pressure for a day we organized the third great demonstration on the last of July when a petition signed by hundreds of thousands of citizens was brought to the Senate asking that body to pass the national suffrage amendment. Women from all parts of the country mobilized in the countryside of
65 Maryland. The delegation motored in gaily decorated automobiles to Washington and went to the Senate, where the entire day was given over to suffrage discussion.

Twenty-two senators spoke in favor of the amendment. Three spoke against it. For the first time in twenty-six years suffrage was actually debated in
70 Congress. That day was historic.

1. One of the main purposes of the passage is to:

   A. expose Woodrow Wilson's opposition to women's suffrage.
   B. describe how the amendment for women's suffrage was passed in Congress.
   C. demonstrate the unjust treatment of suffragists by the government.
   D. show how the persistence of the suffragists brought the suffrage debate to government.

2. The author's point of view is that of:

   F. a feminist historian.
   G. an opponent of women's suffrage.
   H. a participant in the events described.
   J. a leader of the deputation that met with the president.

3. The implication of the police chief's retirement in lines 24–26 is that:

   A. he manhandled some of the parading suffragists.
   B. he was ultimately responsible for the lack of protection at the parade.
   C. the government publicly laid the blame on his shoulders.
   D. he opposed the exoneration of the police force.

4. The author most likely uses the comparison of the suffragists' meeting with the president to a classroom in order to suggest that:

   F. the president planned to teach the suffragists.
   G. the president sought to intimidate the suffragists through a show of force.
   H. the White House staff thought the suffragists were schoolchildren.
   J. the president and his staff treated the suffragists in a condescending manner.

5. According to the passage, President Wilson's initial response to the deputation of suffragists was one of:

   A. sympathetic concern.
   B. intellectual consideration.
   C. naive bewilderment.
   D. disinterested disdain.

THE SCIENCE TEST

DIRECTIONS: After reading the passage, you should select the answer choice that best answers each question. Calculator use is not permitted.

If left at rest, a spring will hang at its equilibrium position. If a mass (M) is attached to that spring, the spring will grow in length by a distance known as its displacement (x). A larger mass will create a larger displacement than a small mass.

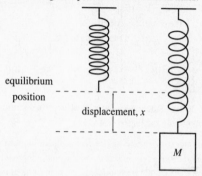

The force (F), in newtons (N), required to return the spring to its equilibrium position is the negative product of the displacement (x) and a spring constant (k), where the negative indicates the direction, not the value, of the force. The spring constant measures the elasticity of a spring: If a spring has a high k, the spring cannot be stretched easily; if a spring has a low k, it can be stretched more easily.

Various masses were attached to two springs with different spring constants, and the force was measured in each of these trials. The energy used (J) returning the spring to its equilibrium position, or Potential Energy (PE), was also measured.

Table 1

Trial	Spring Constant, k	Displacement, x (m)	Force on spring, F (N)	Potential Energy, PE (J)	Mass, M (g)
1	5	1	5	2.5	M_1
2	5	5	25	62.5	M_2
3	5	10	50	250	M_3
4	10	1	10	5	M_4
5	10	5	50	125	M_5
6	10	10	100	500	M_6

1. Which of the following statements about displacement and the force on the spring is consistent with the data in Table 1?

   A. The force on the spring increases as displacement increases.
   B. The force on the spring decreases as displacement increases.
   C. The force on the spring does not change as displacement increases.
   D. The force on the spring increases then decreases as displacement increases.

2. According to the information provided in the introduction and Table 1, which of the following is the largest mass?

   F. M_1
   G. M_3
   H. M_5
   J. M_6

3. If Trial 2 were repeated with a spring with $k = 15$, the displacement of the spring would be:

   A. less than 5.
   B. 5.
   C. between 5 and 15.
   D. greater than 15.

4. Which of the following graphs best represents the change in potential energy with increasing displacement for Trials 1–3?

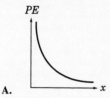

A.

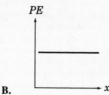

B.

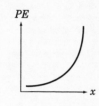

C.

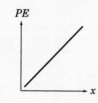

D.

5. What would be the best method of determining how the spring constant affects displacement?

    A. Reproduce Trials 1–6 but use only springs with spring constant $k = 5$.

    B. Reproduce Trials 1–3.

    C. Reproduce Trials 4–6.

    D. Reproduce Trials 1–6 but change the masses in Trials 4–6 to M_1, M_2, and M_3, respectively.

ANSWER KEY

THE ENGLISH TEST

1. B   **4.** H
2. H   **5.** A
3. B

THE MATH TEST

1. D   **4.** J
2. J   **5.** D
3. C

THE READING TEST

1. D   **4.** J
2. H   **5.** D
3. B

THE SCIENCE TEST

1. A   **4.** H
2. J   **5.** D
3. A

PLAN YOUR ATTACK

Now that you've gotten a taste of the questions on each of the ACT Subject Tests, stop to think how you might best budget your time in the days and/or week ahead. Full explanations to each of the mini-test questions are contained in the Intensives, but feel free to skip material on question types you feel you have under control. Or dive right in at the beginning and see how far you get—it's up to you.

Our set of ACT Intensives begins in the next chapter with the English Test.

INTENSIVE 1

The English Test

English Test X-ray

Essential Concepts for
Usage/Mechanics Questions

Essential Concepts for
Rhetorical Skills Questions

Essential Strategies

Practice Set

THE ACT ENGLISH TEST GIVES YOU 45 MINUTES TO WORK through 75 questions spread out among five passages. These passages will be laced with grammatical and stylistic errors, and each passage will be followed by 15 questions. That may seem like a large number of questions, a lot of reading, and relatively little time, but the English Test, more than any other ACT Subject Test, assesses what you already know, namely your knowledge of grammar and writing.

This test measures your sense of correct English writing, so you don't have to memorize esoteric grammatical terminology to do well. Our X-ray will show you what the questions look like, and our Essential Concepts will explain exactly what you do need to know to correctly answer the two types of English questions you'll see: Usage/Mechanics and Rhetorical Skills. We'll finish up with a discussion of Essential Strategies and a practice set. Let's begin.

ENGLISH TEST X-RAY

Here's what a typical English passage looks like, along with samples of the two question types. For now, we'll just use them to familiarize you with what you'll encounter on test day and to establish some terminology. Later in this Intensive, we'll show you how to answer them.

DIRECTIONS: There are five passages on this test. You should read each passage once before answering the questions on it. In order to answer correctly, you may need to read several sentences beyond the question.

There are two question formats within the passages. In one format, you will find words and phrases that have been underlined and assigned numbers. These numbers will correspond with sets of alternative words/phrases, given in the right-hand column of the test booklet. From the sets of alternatives, choose the answer choice that works best in context, keeping in mind whether it employs standard written English, whether it gets across the idea of the section, and whether it suits the tone and style of the passage. You will usually be offered the option "NO CHANGE," which you should choose if you think the version found in the passage is best.

In the second format, you will see boxed numbers referring to sections of the passage or to the passage as a whole. In the right-hand column, you will be asked questions about or given alternatives for the sections marked by the boxes. Choose the answer choice that best answers the question or completes the section.

[1] That summer my parents <u>buy</u> me my

                                    1

first bike—my first true love. [2] One day,

I crashed into a tree and broke my leg. [3]

Unfortunately, my control of the bike was not as

great as my enthusiasm for it. [4] I spent all my

afternoons speeding around the neighborhood

blocks. [2]

1. **A.** NO CHANGE
   B. bought
   C. have bought
   D. buys

2. Which of the following provides the most logical ordering of the sentences in the paragraph?
   F. 3, 2, 1, 4
   G. 3, 1, 4, 2
   H. 1, 4, 3, 2
   J. 1, 4, 2, 3

If you memorize the directions now, you can simply skim them on test day, thereby saving you time. The directions are telling you to read the passage (the short paragraph or paragraphs at the beginning) and then find the best answer to the questions that follow. Don't get tripped up by the word *format*: It simply refers to the questions that follow the passage.

As you can see from the X-ray, some material is underlined or boxed. Both the underlines and the boxes will be numbered so you can find the corresponding multiple-choice answers in the right-hand column of the test booklet. Also, the answer choices are labeled either **A–D** (for odd-numbered questions) or **F–J** (for even-numbered questions).

Question Types

The ACT English Test has two question types:

- Usage/Mechanics
- Rhetorical Skills

You'll see both question types on each of the five English Test paragraphs.

USAGE/MECHANICS

This question type deals with the proper use of standard written English. In our X-ray, question 1 is a Usage/Mechanics question. Note that the directions tell you that the "answer choice that works best" should "employ standard written English." Essentially, that means you need to choose the answer that is grammatically correct. The answer choices provide you with four options to replace the underlined word (*buy* in this case). If you select **A**, you would be selecting "NO CHANGE." (The correct answer is **B**.) On test day, you'll see 40 Usage/Mechanics questions.

RHETORICAL SKILLS

This question type tests your ability to refine written English. In our X-ray, question 2 is a Rhetorical Skills question. The boxed number indicates that the question will deal with a large section of the passage, not just a few words. This question asks you to reorganize the sentences of the paragraph in a logical manner. (The correct answer is **H**.) On test day, you'll see 35 Rhetorical Skills questions.

ESSENTIAL CONCEPTS FOR USAGE/MECHANICS QUESTIONS

The term "Usage/Mechanics" sounds intimidating, but it's simply a fancy name for the rules of the English language. In other words, these three topics:

1. Punctuation
2. Basic Grammar and Usage
3. Sentence Structure

Essential Concept #1: Punctuation

Punctuation is the set of marks that shows you how to read and understand sentences. Ten of the 40 Usage/Mechanics questions will test punctuation, including the following:

- Commas
- Apostrophes
- Semicolons
- Colons

COMMAS

Misplaced, misused, and missing commas are the most frequent punctuation offenders on the English Test. Here's how commas work:

Commas Separate Independent Clauses Joined by a Conjunction. An independent clause contains a subject and a verb (an independent clause can be as short as *I am* or *he reads*), and it can function as a sentence on its own. When you see a conjunction (*and, but, for, or, nor, so, yet*) joining independent clauses, a comma should precede the conjunction. For example:

An independent clause contains a subject and a verb, *and* it can function as a sentence on its own.

Lesley wanted to sit outside, *but* it was raining.

Henry could tie the shoe himself, *or* he could ask Amanda to tie his shoe.

In each example, the clauses on both sides of the comma could stand as sentences on their own. With the addition of the comma and conjunction, the two independent clauses become one sentence.

Commas Delineate a Series of Items. A series contains three or more items separated by commas. The items in a series can be either nouns (such as *dog*) or verb phrases (such as *get in the car*). Commas are essentially the structural backbone of a series. For example:

The hungry girl devoured *a chicken, two pounds of pasta, and a chocolate cake.*

When he learned his girlfriend was coming over, Nathaniel *took a shower, brushed his teeth, and cleaned his room.*

The comma follows all but the last item in the series. When using a conjunction, such as *and* or *or*, at the end of the series, remember to precede it with a comma (. . . *brushed his teeth,* **and** *cleaned his room*).

Commas Set Off Dependent Phrases and Clauses from the Main Clause of a Sentence. Unlike independent clauses, dependent phrases and clauses are not sentences in themselves; rather, they serve to explain or embellish the main clause of a sentence. When they appear at the beginning of a sentence, they should be set off from the main clause by a comma. For example:

Scared of monsters, Tina always checked under her bed before going to sleep.

After preparing an elaborate meal for herself, Anne was too tired to eat.

The first example shows a dependent clause (*Scared of monsters*) acting as an adjective modifying *Tina*. The second example shows a dependent clause acting as an adverb.

When an adverbial clause is at the beginning of a sentence, the adverbial clause needs to be set off from the main clause by a comma. Adverbial clauses should also be set off by commas if they appear in the middle of a sentence. However, if an adverbial clause appears at the end of a sentence, you do not need to use a comma. For example:

Anne was too tired to eat *after preparing an elaborate meal for herself.*

Commas Set Off Nonessential Phrases and Clauses. Nonessential phrases are like nonessential adjectives—they embellish nouns without specifying them. Nonessential phrases should be set off from the rest of the sentence by commas. For example:

Everyone voted Carrie, *who is the most popular girl in our class,* prom queen.

The decrepit street sign, *which had stood in our town since 1799,* finally fell down.

When you use nonessential phrases like the two above, you assume that *Carrie* and *the decrepit street sign* do not need any further identification. If you remove the nonessential phrases, you should still be able to understand the sentences.

Restrictive phrases are not set off by commas because they are necessary to understand the modified noun and the sentence as a whole. For example:

The girl *who is sick* missed three days of school.

The dog *that ate the rotten steak* fell down.

If you removed the restrictive phrases (*who is sick* and *that ate the rotten steak*) from these sentences, you would be left wondering "which girl?" and "which dog?" These restrictive phrases are used to identify exactly which girl missed school and exactly which dog fell. Setting off *who is sick* in commas would assume that the girl's identity is never in doubt; there is only one girl who possibly could have missed school. In this case, we know the identity of the girl only because the restrictive phrase specifies *the girl who is sick.*

Commas Set Off Appositives. Appositives are similar to nonessential phrases. An appositive is a phrase that renames or restates the modified noun, usually enhancing it with additional information. For example:

Everyone voted Carrie, *the most popular girl in school,* prom queen.

The dog, *a Yorkshire terrier,* barked at all the neighbors.

In these two examples, *the most popular girl in school* and *a Yorkshire terrier* are appositives used to describe the nouns they modify.

APOSTROPHES

Apostrophes are the second most commonly tested punctuation mark on the English Test. Apostrophes primarily indicate possession, but they also take the place of omitted letters in contractions (for example, *was not* becomes *wasn't* and *it is* becomes *it's*). You will be tested chiefly on your knowledge of the apostrophe's possessive function.

The Possessive and Singular Nouns. A singular noun (for example: *Simon,* the *dog,* the *bottle*) can be made possessive by adding an apostrophe followed by an *s.* For example:

Simon's teacher was in the room.

My mom forgot the *dog's* food.

We removed the *bottle's* label.

The apostrophe follows directly after the noun. If you move the apostrophe after the *s* (for instance, if you write *dogs'* rather than *dog's*), you will change the meaning of the sentence. If you forget the apostrophe altogether, you will make the sentence meaningless.

The Possessive and Plural Nouns. Most plural nouns (for example: the *boys,* the *dogs,* the *bottles*) can be made possessive by adding only an apostrophe. For example:

The *boys'* teacher was in the room.

My mom forgot the *dogs'* food.

We removed the *bottles'* labels.

The apostrophe directly follows plural nouns that end in *s* to make them possessive.

For plural nouns that do not end in *s* (*women, children, people,* etc.), you should treat the plural form as a singular noun (add an apostrophe followed by an *s*). For example:

The *women's* locker room needs to be cleaned.

The *children's* books are downstairs.

The Possessive and Multiple Nouns. Sometimes you'll want to indicate the possessive of more than one noun (*Nick and Nora, Dan and Johann*). The placement of the apostrophe depends on whether the possessors share the possession. For example:

Nick and Nora's dog solves crimes.

Dan's and Johann's socks are dirty.

In the example of Nick and Nora, the dog belongs to both of them, so you treat *Nick and Nora* as a single unit, followed by a single apostrophe and *s*. In the second example, both Dan and Johann have dirty socks, but they don't share the same dirty socks, so you treat *Dan* and *Johann* as separate units, giving each an apostrophe and *s*.

The Possessive and Pronouns. Unlike nouns and proper nouns, the possessive case of pronouns does not use an apostrophe. For example:

The dog chewed on *its* tail.

You should give him *your* wallet.

Don't confuse *its* and *your* with *it's* and *you're*. *Its* is the possessive form of *it*. *It's* is the contraction of *it is*. This can be tricky to remember because you have been trained to associate apostrophes with possession. But when you're dealing with *its* versus *it's*, the apostrophe signals a contraction. The same is true for *their/they're/there* (*their* is the possessive), *your/you're* (*your* is the possessive), and *whose/who's* (*whose* is the possessive).

SEMICOLONS

You'll usually find several questions dealing with semicolons on the English Test. Semicolons are commonly used to separate two related but independent clauses. For example:

Julie ate five brownies; Eileen ate seven.

Josh needed to buy peas; he ran to the market.

In these cases, you can think of the semicolon as a *weak period*. It suggests a short pause before moving on to a related thought, whereas a period suggests a full stop before moving on to a less-related thought. Generally, a period between these independent clauses would work just as well as a semicolon, so the ACT won't offer you a choice between period or semicolon on the English Test. But you may see the semicolon employed as a weak period in an answer choice; in that case, you should know that it is being used correctly.

Semicolons and Transitional Adverbs. Transitional adverbs (*however, also, consequently, nevertheless, thus, moreover, furthermore,* etc.) can join independent clauses. When they do, they should be preceded by a semicolon and followed, most of the time, by a comma. Short adverbs, such as *thus,* do not need a comma. Here are some examples of transitional adverbs in action:

> Joe always raves about soccer; *however,* he always refuses to watch a
> match.

> If you can't go to the prom with me, let me know as soon as possible;
> *otherwise,* I'll resent you and your inability to communicate for the rest
> of my life.

You need to remember that transitional adverbs must be accompanied by semicolons. If you see a transitional adverb on its own or preceded by a comma on the English Test, you should immediately know there's an error

COLONS

Colons are used after complete sentences to introduce related information that usually comes in the form of a list, an explanation, or a quotation. When you see a colon, you should know to expect elaborating information. For example:

> The wedding had all the elements to make it a classic: *the elegant bride,*
> *the weeping mother, and the fainting bridesmaids.*

In this example, the colon is used to introduce a list of classic wedding elements. Without the list following the colon, the sentence can stand alone (*The wedding had all the elements to make it a classic*). By naming the classic elements of a wedding, the list serves mainly to explain and expand upon the independent sentence that precedes it.

Check out this example of another way to use colons:

> The wedding had all the elements to make it a classic: *The elegant bride beamed as her mother wept and as the bridesmaids fainted.*

Here, the clause following the colon also has an explanatory function. In this case, the colon joins two independent clauses, but the clause following the colon is used to explain and expand the first.

Colons can also be used to introduce quotations.

> The mother's exclamation best summed up the wedding: *"If only the bridesmaids hadn't fainted!"*

Here, the colon is used to introduce the mother's exclamation. Make sure the quotation following the colon is related to the sentence.

Colon Rules. Avoid mistakes with colons by following these two rules:

1. A colon should always be preceded by an independent clause.

> **Incorrect:** The ingredients I need to make a cake: flour, butter, sugar, and icing.

> **Correct:** I need several ingredients to make a cake: flour, butter, sugar, and icing.

In the incorrect example, an incomplete sentence precedes the list of items. The sentence should be reworked to create an independent clause before the colon.

2. There should never be more than one colon in a sentence.

Incorrect: He brought many items on the camping trip: a tent, a sleeping bag, a full cooking set, warm clothes, and several pairs of shoes: sneakers, boots, and sandals.

Correct: He brought many items on the camping trip: a tent, a sleeping bag, a full cooking set, warm clothes, sneakers, boots, and sandals.

If you see a sentence that contains more than one colon or lists within lists, the sentence needs to be rephrased.

Essential Concept #2: Basic Grammar and Usage

Twelve of the 40 questions will test your understanding of the rules of Basic Grammar and Usage. The following are the ones that might give you the most trouble:

- Subject-Verb Agreement
- Pronoun-Antecedent Agreement
- Pronoun Cases

SUBJECT-VERB AGREEMENT

Singular verbs must accompany singular subjects, and plural verbs must accompany plural subjects.

Singular: The *man wears* four ties.

His favorite *college is* in Nebraska.

Matt, along with his friends, *goes* to Coney Island.

Plural: The *men wear* four ties each.

His favorite *colleges are* in Nebraska.

Matt and his friends go to Coney Island.

In the first example with Matt, the subject is singular because the phrase *along with his friends* is isolated in commas. But in the second example with Matt, his friends join the action; the subject becomes *Matt and his friends*, calling for the change to a plural verb.

Subject-verb agreement is fairly straightforward, but the ACT may make this concept tricky by putting the subject at one end of the sentence and the verb a mile away. Try the following example:

An audience of thousands of expectant people who have come from afar to listen to live music in an outdoor setting <u>seem</u> terrifying to a 3 nervous performer.	**3.** **A.** NO CHANGE **B.** seems **C.** have seemed **D.** to seem

To answer this question, cross out the junk in the middle that separates the subject (*an audience*) from the verb (*seem*). Remember that the subject of a sentence can never be part of a phrase that begins with *of*. Here's what you're left with:

An audience *seem* terrifying to a nervous performer.

Now you can see what the verb should be:

An audience *seems* terrifying to a nervous performer.

So the correct answer is **B**. If you were stuck, you could have narrowed down your choices by eliminating **C** and **D** because they don't make much sense in the sentence. If you can isolate the subject and the verb, handling subject-verb agreement is relatively simple.

Collective Nouns. Collective nouns (such as *committee, family, group, number,* and *team*) can be either singular or plural. The verb depends on whether the collective noun is being treated as a single unit or as divided individuals. For example:

Singular: *The number* of people living in Florida *varies* from year to year.

Plural: *A number* of people living in Florida *wish* they had voted for someone else.

Singular: *The committee decides* on the annual program.

Plural: *The committee have disagreed* on the annual program.

Indefinite Pronouns. Indefinite pronouns refer to persons or things that have not been specified. Matching indefinite pronouns with the correct verb form can be tough because some indefinite pronouns that seem plural are actually singular. Questions dealing with singular indefinite pronouns are popular with the test makers, so you'd be wise to memorize a few of these pronouns now. The following indefinite pronouns are always singular, and they tend to appear a lot on the English Test:

another	each	nobody
anybody	everybody	no one
anyone	everyone	somebody
anything	everything	someone

All the indefinite pronouns in the list above should be followed by singular verbs. For example:

Anyone over the age of twenty-one *is* eligible to vote in the United States.

Each has its own patch of grass.

If you're used to thinking these pronouns take plural verbs, these sentences probably sound weird to you. Your best bet is to memorize the list above to remember that those pronouns take singular verbs.

You should also be aware that not all indefinite pronouns are singular. Some (for example, *all*, *any*, *none*, and *some*) can be either singular or plural depending on the context of the sentence. Other indefinite pronouns (for example, *both*, *few*, *many*, and *several*) are always plural. The differences among these indefinite pronouns can be very confusing; determining what's right often requires an astute sense of proper English. On test day, trust your ear: If something sounds wrong, it probably is.

Compound Subjects. Most compound subjects (subjects joined by *and*) should be plural. For example:

Kerry and Vanessa live in Nantucket.

The blue bike and the red wagon need repairs.

The reasoning behind this rule is fairly simple: You have multiple subjects, so you need a plural noun. Thus *Kerry and Vanessa **live*** and *the blue bike and the red wagon **need***.

There Is *or* There Are. Whether to use *there is* or *there are* depends on the singularity or plurality of the noun that the phrase is pointing out. If you have five grapes, you should say "There *are* five grapes." If you have a cat, you should say "There *is* a cat." The *is* and the *are* in these sentences are the main verbs, so they must agree with the noun.

Or *and* Nor. If you have singular subjects joined by an *or* or *nor*, the sentence always takes a singular verb. For example:

Either Susannah or Caitlin is going to be in trouble.

If one of the subjects is plural and the other is singular, the verb agrees with the subject closer to it. For example:

Neither the van nor the buses were operating today.

Either the dogs or the cat is responsible for the mess.

Both of these examples contain a singular and a plural subject. The main verb of the sentence is determined by the subject nearest it: In the first example, *buses* is closer to the verb, so the verb is plural, and in the second example, *cat* is closer to the verb, so the verb is singular.

PRONOUN-ANTECEDENT AGREEMENT

An *antecedent* is the word a pronoun refers to later on in the sentence. In the sentence *Richard put on his shoes*, for example, *Richard* is the antecedent to which *his* refers. When the pronoun does not agree in gender or number with its antecedent, there's an agreement error. For example:

Incorrect: Already late for the show, *Mary* couldn't find *their* keys.

Correct: Already late for the show, *Mary* couldn't find *her* keys.

Unless another sentence states that the keys belong to other people, the possessive pronoun should agree in gender and number with *Mary*. As far as we can tell, *Mary* is a singular, feminine noun, so the pronoun should be too.

The example of Mary contained a fairly obvious example of incorrect agreement, but sometimes the agreement error isn't as obvious. In everyday speech, we tend to say *someone lost **their** shoe* rather than *someone lost **his** shoe* or *someone lost **her** shoe* because we don't want to exclude either gender and because *someone lost **his or her** shoe* sounds cumbersome. You can argue in your spare time about whether *they* as a gender-free singular subject pronoun is acceptable, but remember that it's always wrong on the ACT English Test.

Ambiguous Pronouns. You will also run into agreement errors in which the antecedent is unclear. In these cases, the pronoun is ambiguous. We use ambiguous pronouns all the time in everyday speech, but on the test (*you guessed it*) they're wrong. Take a look at this sentence:

Incorrect: Trot told Ted that *he* should get the mauve pants from the sale rack.

This sentence is unclear because we don't know to whom *he* refers. Should Ted get the pants, or should Trot? You should rewrite the original sentence so that all the pertinent information is relayed without confusion or multiple meanings, such as *Trot told Ted that Ted should get the pants.*

PRONOUN CASES

Pronoun case refers to the role of the pronoun in a sentence. There are three cases: nominative, objective, and possessive. You don't need to know the names of these cases, but you do need to know how to use them correctly. Here, we'll briefly describe each case.

The Nominative Case. The nominative case is used when a pronoun is the subject of a sentence—for example, ***I*** *went to the store* and ***They*** *walked to the park*. You should also use a nominative pronoun after any form of *to be*:

Incorrect: It was *me* on the phone.

Correct: It was *I* on the phone.

In English, *to be* is a grammatical equal sign, so when you have a sentence like *It was I on the phone*, you should be able to do this: *It = I*. If that equation holds true, *I* should be able to take the place of *It* in the sentence: *I was on the phone*.

The nominative also follows comparative clauses that usually begin with *as* or *than*. When a pronoun is involved in a comparison, it must match the case of the other pronoun involved. For example:

Incorrect: I'm fatter than *her*, so I'll probably win this sumo wrestling match.

Correct: I'm fatter than *she*, so I'll probably win this sumo wrestling match.

In this sentence, *I* is being compared to *her*. These two pronouns are in different cases, so one of them must be wrong. *I* and *she* are both nominative cases, so *she* is the correct answer.

Another way to approach comparisons is to realize that comparisons usually omit words. For example, it's grammatically correct to say, *Alexis is stronger than Bill,* but that's an abbreviated version of what you're really saying. The long version is, *Alexis is stronger than Bill is.* That last *is* is invisible in the abbreviated version, but you must remember that it's there. Now let's go back to the sumo sentence. As in our Alexis and Bill example, we don't see the word *is* in the comparison, but it's implied.

If you see a comparison using a pronoun and you're not sure if the pronoun is correct, add the implied *is*. In this case, adding *is* leaves us with *I'm fatter than her is.* That's just wrong, so we know that *she* is the correct pronoun in this case.

The Objective Case. As may be obvious from its name, the objective case ise used when the pronoun is the *object* of another part of speech, usually a preposition or a transitive verb (a verb that takes a direct object):

Preposition: She handed the presents *to them.*

Olivia made a cake *for* Emily, Sarah, and *me.*

Between whom did you sit?

Transitive Verb: Harry *gave me* the tickets.

Call me!

Did you *take him* to the movies?

In the second preposition example, two names appear between *for* and *me.* If this confuses you, eliminate *Emily, Sarah, and* to get *Olivia made a cake for me.* Then you'll see that *me* is the correct pronoun case, not *I* (as in

Olivia made a cake for I). This strategy of crossing out intervening words also works in spotting the correct case for an object of a transitive verb.

In informal, spoken English, you will not hear *whom* used frequently, but in written English (particularly written ACT English), you must remember the all-important *m*. As in the third preposition example, *between whom* is correct; *between who* is not. A good way to figure out if you should use *who* or *whom* in a sentence is to see whether the sentence would use *he* or *him* (or *they* or *them*) if it were rearranged a little. If the sentence takes *he* or *they*, you should use *who*; if it takes *him* or *them*, you should use *whom*.

If you rearrange *Between whom did you sit?* and substitute *them* for *whom*, you get:

Did you sit between them?

This makes it clear that you need to use *whom* in the original sentence.

The Possessive Case. You already know to use the possessive case when indicating possession of an object:

My car

Her dress

Its tail

Whose wheelbarrow

You should also use the possessive case before a gerund, a verb form that usually ends with *ing* and is used as a noun. For example:

When it comes to *my studying* for the ACT, "concentration" is my middle name.

Despite hours of practice, *her playing* is really terrible.

You can think of gerunds as verbs turned magically into nouns, so they need to be preceded by the same possessive pronouns that precede noun objects.

Now that you know something about pronoun cases, try the following sample question:

<u>Me and Jesse</u> went to Cosmic Bowling Night 4 at the Bowladrome.	**4.**	**F.** NO CHANGE **G.** Jesse and me **H.** Jesse and I **J.** I and Jesse

Knowing when to use *I* and when to use *me* can be difficult, especially within compound nouns. If you're not sure which is correct, use the crossing-out trick: Cross out *and Jesse* and see what you have left.

Me went to Cosmic Bowling Night at the Bowladrome.

That sentence sounds (and is) wrong. Here's the correct sentence:

Jesse and I went to Cosmic Bowling Night at the Bowladrome.

So the answer is **H. J**, which also contains the correct pronoun *I*, is wrong because the conventional rules of grammar require that you put yourself after other people in the sentence. *I* should always come after the other people involved in the activity.

Essential Concept #3: Sentence Structure

Of the 40 Usage/Mechanics questions, 18 of them will test your knowledge of sentence structure, the following two topics in particular:

- Sentence Fragments
- Comma Splices

SENTENCE FRAGMENTS

Sentence fragments are incomplete sentences that tend to look like this on the English Test:

Tommy could not pay for his lunch. *Having spent his last dollars on sunglasses.*

Always a bit shy. She found herself unable to talk to the other kids.

These sentence fragments are not sentences on their own. They can be attached to the independent clauses next to them to form complete sentences:

Having spent his last dollars on sunglasses, Tommy could not pay for his lunch.

Always a bit shy, she found herself unable to talk to the other kids.

The answer choices will often make clear whether you should incorporate a fragment into a neighboring sentence:

We didn't go <u>outside. Even</u> though the rain	7.	A. NO CHANGE
7		B. outside;
had stopped.		C. outside; even
		D. outside, even

Notice how **B**, **C**, and **D** all give you the option of combining two sentences into one. That should give you a good clue as to what's required. The variation between the last three choices occurs in punctuation. If you agree that **A** is incorrect, you can rely on your punctuation skills to decipher the correct answer. The answer is **D** because **B** and **C**, with their use of the semicolon, continue to isolate the sentence fragment from the sentence.

Other sentence fragment questions will ask you to turn a fragment into its own full sentence rather than simply to incorporate it into a different sentence. Again, you'll be able to tell from the answer choices what the ACT wants:

We didn't go outside. <u>While the</u> rain continued	8.	F. NO CHANGE
8		G. Although the
to fall.		H. The
		J. Since the

F, **G**, and **J** don't solve the sentence fragment problem. By choosing those, you still end up with a subordinate clause posing as a sentence (**G** and **J** simply replace one subordinating conjunction with another). But by getting rid of the subordinating conjunction altogether, you form a real sentence: *The rain continued to fall.* The correct answer is **H**.

COMMA SPLICES

A comma splice occurs when two independent clauses are joined together by a comma with no intervening conjunction. For example:

> Bowen walked to the *park, Leah* followed behind.

The comma between *park* and *Leah* forms a comma splice. Although the sentence may sound correct because the comma demands a short pause between the two related clauses, the structure is wrong in written English. There are three ways to fix a comma splice:

1. Use a semicolon.
> Bowen walked to the *park; Leah* followed behind.

2. Separate the clauses into two sentences.
> Bowen walked to the *park. Leah* followed behind.

3. Add a conjunction.
> Bowen walked to the *park, while Leah* followed behind.
> Bowen walked to the *park, and Leah* followed behind.

Inserting *while* subordinates the "Leah" clause to the "Bowen" clause. In the second sentence, the *and* joins the two clauses on equal footing.

ESSENTIAL CONCEPTS FOR RHETORICAL SKILLS QUESTIONS

Like "Usage/Mechanics," "Rhetorical Skills" is another doozy of a name. But these questions simply test your ability to recognize proper writing. You'll see questions on three major topics:

1. Writing Strategy
2. Organization
3. Style

Some people may find the Rhetorical Skills questions more challenging than the Usage/Mechanics questions because the rules are not as concrete. Others may find them easier for that very reason.

Essential Concept #1: Writing Strategy

Writing strategy involves improving the effectiveness of a passage through careful revision and editing. You'll sometimes have to choose the best option for strengthening an argument by adding topic sentences, transitions, information, or evidence. In other questions, you may have to choose which sections of an argument can be deleted, or you might have to identify the purpose of a passage—its audience or its message.

To sum up, 12 of the 35 Rhetorical Skills questions will cover Writing Strategy by asking questions about these topics:

- Transitions and Topic Sentences
- Additional Detail and Evidence
- Big Picture/Purpose

We'll show you how the ACT tests your grasp of topics by working through some sample questions.

TRANSITIONS AND TOPIC SENTENCES

These questions ask you to figure out the best way to open or conclude paragraphs within a passage. A *topic sentence* begins a paragraph, very specifically strengthening the focus and introducing a concrete topic. A *transition sentence* needs to refer to something previously mentioned while also introducing new information (this means it needs to be able to do two things). Here's an example:

[2]

Victorian novelists were often concerned with issues of character, plot, and the Victorian social world. Dickens's novels, for example, were several-hundred-page-long works documenting the elaborate inter-weaving of his characters.

[3]

5 Their "modernist" novels to tended focus on the characters' inner lives, which they depicted through a stylistic technique called "stream of consciousness." Several of the best-known modernist novels were written in this stream-of-consciousness style. 6

5. The writer wishes to begin Paragraph 3 with a sentence that strengthens the focus of the paragraph, while providing a transition from Paragraph 2. Which of the following would be the best choice?

A. In the early twentieth century, novelists began to reject the Victorian emphasis on social context and look for a new focus for the novel.

B. Victorian novels ended with the Victorian era.

C. In the early twentieth century, novelists further developed this emphasis on characters' inner lives.

D. World War I significantly affected British culture in the twentieth century.

This question asks you to choose a sentence that will simultaneously serve to strengthen the focus of the paragraph (what we call a "topic sentence") for Paragraph 3 and as a transition sentence between the two paragraphs. We're looking for one sentence that's both specific and talks about two ideas. In order to answer this question correctly, you need to understand what the two paragraphs are saying. We suggest that you reread Paragraph 3 first. By developing a good sense of what that paragraph says, you can eliminate answer choices that clearly do not work as topic sentences.

B talks exclusively about the Victorian novel, making it an inappropriate topic sentence for a paragraph on modernist novels. **D** doesn't talk specifically about novels at all. Its focus is World War I, which is not mentioned elsewhere in the paragraph. Eliminate them both. So now you've narrowed the selection down to **A** and **C**. These sentences have similar constructions, but they say radically different things: **A** claims that twentieth-century novelists rejected Victorian ideas, while **C** claims that they embraced and developed Victorian ideas. In order to figure out which one of these claims is true, you need to have read Paragraph 2 in addition to Paragraph 3.

Paragraph 2 tells you that Victorian novelists were primarily concerned with the social world. In Paragraph 3, you discover that modernist novelists were primarily concerned with characters' thoughts and inner lives. Thus Paragraph 3 describes a change in novel writing that occurred between the Victorian era and the early twentieth century. The correct answer to the question is **A**.

Sometimes you'll be asked to select only a topic sentence or only a transition sentence from the answer choices. Those questions are usually less complex than the example above because you have to perform one fewer step. You may also be asked to choose a concluding sentence for a paragraph. These questions are similar to transition questions because a good concluding sentence tends to be one that easily and sensibly makes the transition to the next paragraph.

ADDITIONAL DETAIL AND EVIDENCE

These questions ask you to flesh out a paragraph by selecting the answer choice that provides the best additional detail or evidence. "Additional detail" means specific details that have not previously been introduced but which relate very closely to the topic and follow the same line of thought without digressing or contradicting the previous mood or information. For example:

[3]

⑤ Their "modernist" novels to tended focus on the characters' inner lives, which they depicted through a stylistic technique called "stream of consciousness." Several of the best-known modernist novels were written in this stream-of-consciousness style. ⑥

6. The writer wishes to add information here that will further support the point made in the preceding sentence. Which of the following sentences will do that best?

F. Today, this style is not as popular as it once was.

G. However, there are many famous early twentieth-century works not written in this style.

H. Joyce's *Ulysses*, for example, was written in this style, and it is widely considered one of the most important books of the century.

J. Ford's *The Good Soldier*, although less read today, is a great example of this style.

F talks about the popularity of this style among contemporary authors—an issue that the preceding sentence does not address. You can eliminate **G** almost immediately because it starts with *however*, which indicates that it is going to make a statement that attempts to contradict, not support, the previous point.

Now you've successfully limited the choices to **H** and **J**. Both would provide the paragraph with an example of a stream-of-consciousness work. The key to deciding which of these sentences is correct lies in the preceding sentence, which talks about the "best-known modernist novels." On the one hand, **J** tells you that *The Good Soldier* is "less read today" and also, presumably, less well known. On the other hand, **H** tells you that *Ulysses* is "widely considered one of the most important books of the century." This statement suggests that the novel is famous, so **H** is correct.

BIG PICTURE/PURPOSE

Big Picture/Purpose questions always come at the end of a passage, and they ask you to look at the *big picture*—hence the name—and identify a passage's main point, intended purpose, or intended audience. (Purpose and main idea will come up again, in the Reading Test Intensive.) The English Test questions on this concept will often be phrased as follows:

9. Suppose the writer has been assigned to write an essay explaining the development of the British novel from 1799 to 1945. Would this essay successfully fulfill the assignment?

The answer choices to these questions come in two parts: The first part will respond either "no" or "yes" to the question, and the second part will give an explanation for this answer. For example:

A. No, because the essay restricts its focus to the American novel from 1850 to 1945.

B. No, because the essay omits mention of famous poets.

C. Yes, because the essay focuses on the novel's birth in the eighteenth century.

D. Yes, because the essay describes changes in novel writing from the end of the French Revolution to the end of World War II.

Without reading the entire passage, you're probably unable to answer a definite "no" or "yes" to this question, but you can eliminate an incorrect answer or two because of irrelevant or nonsensical explanations. In this example, you can immediately cross off **B** because the explanation calls for a discussion of famous poets in the essay. Famous poets, however, do not necessarily belong in an essay on the novel's development. You can also cross off **C**. It claims that the passage *successfully* fulfills the essay requirements because it discusses the novel's birth in the eighteenth century. However, the assignment calls for a discussion of the novel starting in 1799 (the end of the eighteenth century), so **C** cannot be correct.

By reading and understanding the passage, you'll be able to choose from the two remaining answers. If the passage indeed focuses on the American novel, **A** is correct, and the essay does not succeed; if the essay describes the novel from the end of the French Revolution (1799) to the end of World War II (1945), **D** is correct, and the essay does succeed.

But if you were pressed for time, or had trouble understanding the passage, you could still narrow down the answer choices, as we've done here. Because the ACT doesn't have a wrong-answer penalty, you're always better off guessing, rather than leaving a question blank. If you can eliminate just one or even two answer choices, you've already significantly upped your changes of guessing the correct answer from those that remain.

Essential Concept #2: Organization

Organization questions deal with the logical structuring of the passage on the level of the sentence, the paragraph, and the passage as a whole. You'll see approximately 11 of these on the English Test. These questions want you to reorganize sections to maximize their coherence, order, and unity. You'll need to do this on three different levels:

- Sentence Reorganization
- Paragraph Reorganization
- Passage Reorganization

SENTENCE REORGANIZATION

Sentence reorganization often involves the placement of a modifier within a sentence. Here's an example:

Austen wrote about a society of manners, in which love triumphs over a rigid social hierarchy <u>despite confinement to her drawing room.</u> 10	**10. F.** NO CHANGE **G.** (Place after *love*) **H.** (Place after *Austen*) **J.** (Place after *society*)

This question tests whether you can identify and correct a *misplaced modifier*. A phrase should be right next to the word it modifies. In this example, *despite confinement to her drawing room* modifies *Austen*, so the phrase needs to be right after *Austen*. The correct answer is **H**.

PARAGRAPH REORGANIZATION

A couple of questions will ask you to reorder sentences within a paragraph. They'll look much like this:

[1] In April, I'm usually in a bad mood because of my debilitating pollen allergies. [2] In November, despite the graying trees and the short days, I'm elated because I can celebrate both Thanksgiving and my birthday. [3] My mood changes with the months. [4] In the summer months I feel happy from days spent in the sun. [11]

11. Which of the following provides the most logical ordering of the sentences in the preceding paragraph?

A. 1, 4, 3, 2
B. 3, 4, 2, 1
C. 3, 1, 4, 2
D. 2, 1, 4

The best way to approach these questions is to decide which sentence should come first and then eliminate incompatible answer choices. Ask yourself which sentence logically comes first in this sequence. Sentence 3 makes a good topic sentence because it provides an argument that can be followed and supported by examples. By deciding that Sentence 3 should come first, you can immediately eliminate **A** and **D** because they do not begin with Sentence 3. Now you can move on to arranging the rest of the paragraph. Each of the remaining sentences talks about a different time of year: April, summer, and November. The three sentences should fall in that chronological order (April, summer, November), as it is the most logical arrangement in this example. Therefore, the correct answer is **C**.

If you're totally lost on a paragraph reorganization question, mine the answer choices for clues. You can look at the first sentences given to you by the answer choices and see whether any of them sound like topic sentences.

If you can identify a topic sentence, you're well on your way to getting the correct answer.

PASSAGE REORGANIZATION

These questions appear at the end of passages and ask you either to insert a sentence where it best belongs in the passage or to move a paragraph to a different location in the passage. Questions that ask you to insert a sentence will generally look like this:

---

12. The writer wishes to include the following sentence in the essay:

> That summer, I spent so much time on the beach that I could smell only a combination of sand and seaweed when I finally returned to school.

That sentence will fit most smoothly and logically into Paragraph:

F. 2, before the first sentence.
G. 3, after the last sentence.
H. 4, before the first sentence.
J. 5, after the last sentence.

This question asks you to identify the sentence provided as an appropriate topic or concluding sentence for Paragraphs 2, 3, 4, or 5. When the answer choice calls for the sentence to be placed "before the first sentence," then it would become the topic sentence of the paragraph. When the answer choice calls for the sentence to be placed "after the last sentence," then it would become the concluding sentence. A topic sentence focuses the paragraph's topic, and a concluding sentence follows logically from and sums up the paragraph it ends, so you should look for the paragraph that most closely relates to the sentence.

Questions that ask you to relocate a paragraph will generally look like this:

---

13. For the sake of the unity and coherence of this essay, Paragraph 4 should be placed:

    A. where it is now.
    B. after Paragraph 1.
    C. after Paragraph 2.
    D. after Paragraph 5.

To answer this question, look at (and perhaps underline) the topic sentences of each paragraph. They provide an outline of the passage and should follow a logical chain of thought. For example, look at these topic sentences:

Topic Sentence 1: Seasonal variations affect many aspects of my life.

Topic Sentence 2: This April, the sight of leaves and the sounds of returning birds cheered me so much that I hugged a tree.

Topic Sentence 3: The return of the warm weather also meant that I got some much-needed exercise after being stuck indoors all winter.

Topic Sentence 4: My mood changes with the months.

Topic Sentence 5: The weather's effect on my mood and my fitness always reminds me of the undeniable connection between people and nature.

Even without reading the whole passage, you can take an educated stab at the correct answer. Consider the logical organization of an essay: introduction, supporting paragraphs, and conclusion. According to this structure,

Topic Sentence 1 should present the passage's argument, and it should be followed by three paragraphs supporting the argument and a final paragraph presenting a conclusion.

Now take a look at Topic Sentence 4. It makes a general argument about the weather's effect on the author's mood. Ask yourself where the paragraph best fits into the passage: Is it a supporting paragraph or a conclusion? It's unlikely that Paragraph 4 is a conclusion because it narrows the focus of the essay to talk about the author's mood, while other paragraphs in the essay discuss the author's physical condition. Eliminating **D** (which would make it the conclusion) leaves you with three options for a supporting paragraph.

Next you should be to take a look at the remaining topic sentences. Topic Sentence 2 also discusses the weather's effect on the author's mood, but it deals specifically with April weather. Topic Sentence 3 discusses the weather's effects on the author's physical health. If you choose **A** and keep Paragraph 4 where it is, the passage will be ordered like this: introduction, weather/mood, weather/health, weather/mood, conclusion. This order doesn't make much sense because it inexplicably divides the weather/mood discussions. Eliminate **A**. **B** puts Paragraph 4 (general weather/mood) before Paragraph 2 (April weather/mood), while **C** puts 2 before 4. When writing an essay, moving from the general to the specific makes more sense than moving in the opposite direction because you want to support your claims with specific evidence. The correct answer is **B**.

If you get stumped on a question that asks you to reorganize the paragraphs within a passage, don't panic. Instead, take a quick scan through the topic sentences of each paragraph, and let their content guide you, as we've done here. Remember too that the ACT will always want you to make the most logical revisions possible, which means keeping like ideas with like ideas.

Essential Concept #3: Style

Style questions generally concern effective word choice. They often ask you to eliminate redundant words or choose the most appropriate word for a sentence in terms of its tone and clarity. Twelve of the 35 Rhetorical Skills questions will test style, with questions about:

- Redundancy
- Word Choice and Tone

REDUNDANCY

The ACT will test your ability to spot redundant statements. Redundant statements say the same thing twice, and you should always avoid redundancy on the English Test (in life too, if possible). For example:

Incorrect: The diner closes at 3 AM in the morning.

Correct: The diner closes at 3 AM.

In the morning is redundant because it is implied in *AM*. Here's another example of a redundant statement:

In my opinion, I think we should go get some food.

I think and *In my opinion* mean the same thing, so you can eliminate one of the phrases from the sentence.

Redundancy questions almost always give you the option to "OMIT the underlined portion." If you spot a phrase or word that means the same thing as the underlined portion, then you should always choose to "OMIT."

WORD CHOICE AND TONE

Identifying the appropriate word choice can be as simple as figuring out whether a sentence should use the word *their, there,* or *they're.* But word choice can also be more complicated, involving many words working together to create a tone. For example, the sentence *Lloyd George rocks!* probably does not belong in an essay on World War I. It doesn't fit because it's written in a casual, slangy tone, and history essays are generally neither casual nor slangy. The sentence might belong, however, in a passage on your awesome new friend, Lloyd George.

The content of a passage will generally give you a clue about the appropriate tone. Essays on history and culture will probably be written in a fairly formal style—a style that omits youthful slang, casual contractions, and familiar personal pronouns (such as *I* and *you*). A personal essay on your experiences driving a bulldozer, your great-grandmother, or your new skateboard calls for a relatively informal style of writing. Tone is one of the most important elements in correctly answering word choice questions. You will encounter quite a few questions that look like this:

During the Great War, the British public believed that Lloyd George <u>rocks!</u> He was widely admired 14 for his ability to unify the government and thus to unify Britain.	**14. F.** NO CHANGE **G.** rocked! **H.** was an effective political leader. **J.** had the ability to unify

Because we already told you that informality does not belong in a history essay, you can immediately eliminate **F** and **G**, even though **G** correctly changes the verb tense. If you read the section on page 60, you should also be able to eliminate **J** because it is redundant—it repeats the information given in the next sentence. That leaves the correct answer, **H**.

ESSENTIAL STRATEGIES

As we discussed in the X-ray, the ACT intersperses Usage/Mechanics questions and Rhetorical Skills questions within the same passage. You might have realized that the two question formats sometimes even look alike, though they test different skills. The order of the questions depends on what part of the passage is being referred to: A question at the beginning deals with the beginning of the passage, a question in the middle deals with the middle of the passage, and so on.

In this section, we give you the strategies to use on both question types.

So, without further ado, let's take a look:

- Read the Entire Passage First
- Use Process of Elimination
- Choose "NO CHANGE" or "OMIT"

Now we'll see how these strategies work.

Read the Entire Passage First

Don't immediately jump to the questions. Instead, first read quickly through the passage you're working on, then begin answering the accompanying questions.

While reading the passage once through before getting to the questions may seem like extra work, it will prevent you from making unnecessary errors and gives you an understanding of the passage's purpose, argument, and tone, which are important to keep in mind when answering Rhetorical Skills questions.

The English Test instructions warn that you may need to read beyond a question in order to answer it correctly. If you need further convincing, the following sample English Test question demonstrates why reading beyond the underlined section is necessary:

her dogs <u>has</u> sleek, brown hair 15	**15.** **A.** NO CHANGE **B.** are **C.** have **D.** do not have

"Ah, a simple subject-verb agreement problem," you're probably thinking. "The answer, obviously, is **C**." But what if we show you the whole sentence?

The girl walking her dogs <u>has</u> sleek, 15 brown hair	**15.** **A.** NO CHANGE **B.** are **C.** have **D.** do not have

Reading the rest of the sentence reveals that the sleek, brown hair belongs to a girl rather than a pack of dogs. The question was about subject-verb agreement, but the words directly next to the underlined phrase misled you into thinking that the subject was *her dogs* and not *the girl*. If you had read the passage first, you would have realized that the correct answer is **A**.

Admittedly, this example exaggerates the case for reading beyond the question, but it gets our point across. Ultimately, if you quickly read through the passage before tackling the questions, you'll avoid unnecessary mistakes without sacrificing much time.

Use Process of Elimination

In the Introduction, we discussed guessing intelligently. Whenever you guess, try first to eliminate some answers to improve your odds. Take a look at these sample answers:

A. When I swung the bat I knew, I had hit a home run.
B. When I swung the bat, I knew I had hit a home run.
C. When I swing the bat I know I will always hit a home run.
D. When, I swung the bat I knew, I had hit a home run.

You can probably figure out from these answer choices that there is a comma placement error. **A**, **B**, and **D** all give versions of the same sentence with different comma placement. **C**, attempting to lure you off the right track, offers a comma-less version of the sentence with altered verb tenses.

See if you can you eliminate any of these answer choices. **C** looks like a prime candidate for elimination because it makes little sense in context. **D** also looks like it can go because of the comma placed after *When*, which leaves the word dangling at the beginning of the sentence. If you can eliminate either or both of these, you greatly increase the chance that you'll pick the correct answer, which is **B**.

CHOICES WITH MULTIPLE ERRORS

Instead of tackling all the errors at once, you'll have an easier time picking them off one by one. Let's use the following example:

A. Cathys' friends left they're bags in the room.
B. Cathy's friends left there bags in the room.
C. Cathys friends left their bags in the room.
D. Cathy's friends left their bags in the room.

These sentences contain two variations. If you focus on Cathy and her friends, you realize that you should eliminate **A** and **C** for incorrect apostrophe placement. Now you've narrowed your options to **B** and **D**, which respectively use *there* and *their* as possessive pronouns. If you don't know the difference between the two, you have a 50 percent chance of guessing the right answer. If you do know the difference, you know that *there bags* is incorrect and that the correct answer is therefore **D**.

CHOICES THAT OVERCORRECT

Be wary of answer choices that try to trick you into overcorrecting the problem. Don't be fooled into finding additional "errors" by an answer choice that has completely made over the original.

Choose "NO CHANGE" or "OMIT"

All Usage/Mechanics questions offer you "NO CHANGE" as an answer choice. Do not overlook "NO CHANGE" as a possible answer to the problem. It is correct approximately 20 percent of the time it's offered. If your gut tells you there's nothing wrong with the underlined phrase, don't change the phrase.

You will also often see the answer choice "OMIT the underlined portion." By choosing it, you can remove the entire underlined portion from the passage.

When an answer choice allows you to "OMIT the underlined portion," think hard about that option. "OMIT," when it appears as an answer, is correct approximately 25 percent of the time. "OMIT" is an attractive (and often correct) answer because it eliminates redundant or irrelevant statements. Here's an example:

The bag was free. <u>I didn't have to pay for it.</u>
16

16. **F.** I paid for it.
  G. I paid five dollars for it.
  H. I paid almost nothing for it.
  J. OMIT the underlined portion.

The ACT writers want your edits to make the passage as concise as possible. A statement like the one above should strike you as redundant because you clearly don't need to pay for something that's free—so why say the same thing twice? **J** is correct.

PRACTICE SET

Try this mix of Usage/Mechanics and Rhetorical Skills questions to see where you stand. Don't forget to read through the explanations that follow.

PASSAGE I

Area 51

[1]

For believers and conspiracy theorists

in alien life forms, Area 51 is a dream
           1

come true. Not only have their been
                           2

numerous alien sightings, and the
                        3

government has until recently, denied
                 4

the existence of the Area. Area 51 which
                              5

is ninety-five miles north of Las Vegas,

is a piece of government-owned land that

includes an Air Force base.

Which is off-limits to most pilots,
      6

including military pilots.

1. **A.** NO CHANGE
   B. (place after *for*)
   C. (place after *believers*)
   D. (place after *conspiracy*)

2. **F.** NO CHANGE
   G. they're been
   H. there been
   J. they are being

3. **A.** NO CHANGE
   B. since
   C. yet
   D. but

4. **F.** NO CHANGE
   G. has, until recently,
   H. has until, recently,
   J. have until recently

5. **A.** NO CHANGE
   B. Area 51 that
   C. Area 51, which
   D. Area 51, that

6. **F.** NO CHANGE
   G. The Air Force base is
      off-limits
   H. That is off-limits
   J. And it is off-limits

[1] Tourists flock to Area 51. [2] They hope to catch a glimpse of UFOs, and they often get lucky, there have been
₇
innumerable reported sightings of everything from flying saucers to actual aliens. [3] The so-called "Cammo Dudes" is one favorite tourist attraction; they are
₈
men who patrol the Area in unmarked camouflage uniforms and white Jeeps. [4] Many of the UFO sightings are described as strange lights in the sky. [5] Problematically for believers in alien life, these strange
₉
flashes of light can be explained: The government uses Area 51 to test new aircraft a practice that can result in
₁₀
sudden and seemingly inexplicable flashes of light. [11]

7. **A.** NO CHANGE
   B. lucky that there
   C. lucky; there
   D. lucky:

8. **F.** NO CHANGE
   G. are
   H. was
   J. were

9. **A.** NO CHANGE
   B. For problematically believers in alien life
   C. It is for believers, problematically, in alien life,
   D. Believers, problematically for them in alien life

10. **F.** NO CHANGE
    G. aircraft; a practice
    H. aircraft, a practice
    J. aircraft: a practice

11. Which of the sentences in Paragraph 2 should be eliminated?
    A. 1
    B. 3
    C. 4
    D. 5

[3]

Another difficulty for believers is that while many tourists claim to see almost limitless <u>and immeasurable</u> numbers
12
of alien aircraft, many people who live near Area 51 have never seen a single alien or alien craft.

[4]

But even if those who believe in alien life forms are disappointed, the conspiracy theorists still have something to cling to. The government is <u>real secretive</u> about
13
the Air Force base. They do not like to discuss it in the media, <u>but</u> they closed two
14
spots where previously the public was allowed to view the base.

12. **F.** and: immeasurable
G. and, immeasurable
H. and innumerable
J. OMIT the underlined portion

13. **A.** NO CHANGE
B. real secret
C. really secretive
D. very secret

14. **F.** NO CHANGE
G. yet
H. and
J. furthermore

Question 15 asks about the essay as a whole.

15. Does it seem that the writer of this essay believes in aliens?

A. Yes, the writer expresses a firm belief in alien life forms.

B. No, the writer is openly scornful of those who believe in aliens.

C. Yes, the writer hints at a tentative belief in life on other planets.

D. No, the writer seems not to believe in aliens.

PASSAGE II
John Adams:
The Comeback Kid?
[1]

Interest in John Adams has been

getting increasingly more intense since the
16

publication of books about him by David

McCullough and Joseph J. Ellis.

[2]

In the past, Adams had been neglected
17

in favor of other founding fathers such

as Thomas Jefferson. When McCullough

began his book on Adams, he wanted it

to be about both Adams and Jefferson,

and he wondered if Jefferson would

overshadow Adams? [19] But as he wrote,
18

he began to feel that Adams was actually

superior to Thomas Jefferson in political

achievements and in moral fiber.

16. **F.** NO CHANGE
    G. getting more and more
        intense
    H. growing intenser by the
        minute
    J. intensifying

17. **A.** NO CHANGE
    B. is
    C. would have been
    D. were

18. **F.** NO CHANGE
    G. overshadow, Adams?
    H. overshadow Adams.
    J. overshadow Adams . . .

19. Which of the following
phrases should be added at the
beginning of the preceding
sentence in order to make the
progression of ideas more
understandable?

    A. And so,
    B. Because
    C. Therefore,
    D. In fact,

[3]

McCullough writes that Adams was
the man <u>more</u> responsible for the adoption
20
of independence by the Continental
Congress. It was <u>he</u> who marshaled the
21
requisite number of votes to pass the
measure. Adams also brokered peace with
France, <u>that</u> enabled Thomas Jefferson
22
to complete the Louisiana Purchase.

[4]

Although less important to the
nation, Adams's moral triumphs were as
resounding as his political ones. Adams
passionately loved his wife, Abigail, but
in order to serve the country, he had to
spend almost all of his time away from her.
Government jobs did not pay well, and in

20. **F.** NO CHANGE
    G. the more
    H. most
    J. even more

21. **A.** NO CHANGE
    B. himself
    C. him
    D. they

22. **F.** NO CHANGE
    G. which
    H. who
    J. they

order to make ends meet, <u>the family farm</u>

<u>were run by Abigail.</u> She worked in
23

Massachusetts while her husband worked

in Philadelphia. The letters of the couple

<u>is</u> a testament to the hardship they suffered
24

while apart from one another. <u>There</u>
25

sacrifice was a great one.

[5]

Adams was wonderfully unsentimental

about his country. He <u>objected the</u>
26

idolization of the founding fathers, and never

characterized the Revolution <u>as noble, he saw</u>
27

it as fraught with disagreement, an

enterprise run by ordinary people.

[6]

<u>But</u> John Adams's quick temper and
28

bluntness may have made him unpopular

23. **A.** NO CHANGE
B. the family farm was under the control of Abigail
C. running the family farm was Abigail
D. Abigail ran the family farm

24. **F.** NO CHANGE
G. have
H. are
J. were

25. **A.** NO CHANGE
B. Their
C. They're
D. Her

26. **F.** NO CHANGE
G. objected for the
H. objected at the
J. objected to the

27. **A.** NO CHANGE
B. as noble he saw
C. as noble; he saw
D. as noble, but he saw

28. **F.** Rather
G. So
H. Yet
J. OMIT the underlined portion.

Questions 29 and 30 ask about the essay as a whole.

with some people in his day, but the import

of his deeds has made him more and more

popular in recent years.

29. The writer wants to add one of the following closing sentences. Which is most appropriate, considering the essay as a whole?

  A. He might have had a bad temper, but in the final analysis it does not matter.

  B. Adams was the founding father perhaps most responsible for our country as we know it.

  C. Adams was one of the most important founding fathers, and he seems to be becoming one of the best-loved too.

  D. He was one of the only elder statesmen capable of examining our country and our history in an objective way.

30. The writer wishes to include the following sentence in order to further clarify Adams's role:

  Over the course of his career in politics, Adams made contributions that changed the course of American history.

  Where should it be added?

  F. At the beginning of Paragraph 2

  G. At the beginning of Paragraph 3

  H. At the beginning of Paragraph 4

  J. At the beginning of Paragraph 5

Guided Explanations

PASSAGE I

1. C

The original sentence makes it sound as if the believers and theorists are in the shape of alien life forms. By moving the underlined phrase, it becomes clear that we're talking about people who believe in alien life forms.

2. H

There is what's needed because we're talking about a physical location. *Their* is the possessive.

3. D

Typically, a sentence that starts *not only* goes like this: Not only ___, but ___ . The use of *and, since,* or *yet* to begin that second clause is idiomatically incorrect.

4. G

The comma provided by **G** is needed for clarity.

5. C

Again, you need an additional comma for the sake of clarity. Also, in this context, the word *which* should be preceded by a comma.

6. G

The sentence given by **G**, unlike the original sentence, has a subject: the *Air Force base*. **H** and **J** are both sentence fragments.

7. C

The correct answer fixes the problem by placing a semicolon between the two halves of the sentence. Remember that the ACT likes to use the semicolon as a weak period.

8. G

We're talking about plural *Cammo Dudes,* so the verb must be plural. Therefore, the plural *are* is correct. *Was* is singular and the wrong tense, and *were* is the wrong tense.

9. A

No error. As we said in the Essential Strategies section, don't be afraid to choose "NO CHANGE."

10. H

The added comma increases clarity. **G** and **J** use overly strong marks of punctuation. We don't need a full stop here, just a pause.

11. B

The third sentence in this paragraph is unnecessary. The rest of the sentence is about tourists seeing alien phenomena, and the Cammo Dudes aren't aliens; they're humans.

12. J

Because the word *limitless* is already there, *immeasurable* is redundant.

13. C

Real secretive is okay in speech, but not in writing. The adverb *really* is required to describe the adjective *secretive*.

14. H
The last sentence discusses two secretive things. The two things are similar, so they should be joined by *and*, not *but*, which implies a contrast.

15. D
The writer takes an amused, removed tone and discusses the tourists who believe in aliens with a little bit of humor. This implies that he does not believe in aliens. **B** is too strongly worded. The writer is not scornful.

PASSAGE II

16. J
The correct answer connotes the same meaning as the underlined phrase and in half the space.

17. A
The sentence already in the passage is the best choice.

18. H
Even though it mentions a question, this sentence should end in a period, not a question mark, because the sentence itself is declarative: *he wondered.*

19. D
Adding *in fact* smoothes the transition from the first to the second sentence.

20. H
You can't say Adams was *more* responsible, because the sentence doesn't say he was more responsible than someone else. Therefore, grammatically speaking, he must be the *most* responsible.

21. A

No error.

22. G

When you have a non-essential clause, as you do here, use *which*, not *that*.

23. D

The best answer fixes the subject-verb disagreement and eliminates the passive voice.

24. H

The subject is *letters*, which is plural, so the plural verb is correct. **G**'s *have* is nonidiomatic usage, and **J**'s *were* is past tense, which is incorrect, because the letters are a testament currently.

25. B

The writer is talking about a sacrifice made by the couple, so the phrase should be *their sacrifice*.

26. J

English idiom dictates that we *object to* things, not *object them*, *object for* them, or *object at* them.

27. C

The correct answer fixes the run-on by inserting a semicolon between the two independent clauses. **B** is a run-on. **D** solves the problem by adding a connecting word, but that connecting word is illogical.

28. J

The only *but* we need is the second one, which comes after the comma. The writer is trying to contrast the second idea to the first, so the first *but* is inappropriate. Remember: It's okay to "OMIT."

29. C

Only answer **C** refers to the essay as a whole. **A** and **B** are too specific.

30. G

We need to keep like with like when revising. Both this sentence and the third paragraph are about Adam's contributions to politics.

INTENSIVE 2

The Math Test

Math Test X-ray

Essential Concepts

Essential Strategies

Practice Set

THE ACT MATH TEST IS A 60-MINUTE, 60-QUESTION TEST.
It covers six areas of high school math:

- Pre-Algebra
- Elementary Algebra
- Intermediate Algebra
- Coordinate Geometry
- Plane Geometry
- Trigonometry

The majority of questions deal with pre-algebra, elementary algebra, and plane geometry, which are usually covered at the beginning of high school. The other three topics—intermediate algebra, coordinate geometry, and trigonometry—constitute only about a third of the questions on the test. If you haven't yet learned trigonometry, don't sweat it: There are only four trig questions on the test, and four questions won't ruin your score.

Rather than bog you down with every possible equation, formula, or math concept on the ACT, this Intensive gives you the strategies you'll use to solve ACT Math problems. Every practice problem points out the math concepts in play. However, if you come across a concept you don't know, or if you need a refresher, look it up at **www.sparknotes.com/math/primer**. Our online math primer is a resource to help you study any and all topics you may need to review.

The Math Test differs from the other ACT Subject Tests in two significant ways:

1. You're allowed to use a calculator.
2. There are five answer choices for each question, rather than four.

Now let's turn our attention to the X-ray.

MATH TEST X-RAY

On test day, you'll see 60 multiple-choice questions. There are two types of questions:

- Basic problems
- Word problems

Following is an example of each question type, along with the ACT Math Test directions.

DIRECTIONS: After solving each problem, pick the correct answer from the five given and fill in the corresponding oval on your answer sheet. Solve as many problems as you can in the time allowed. Do not worry over problems that take too much time; skip them if necessary and return to them if you have time.

Calculator use is permitted on the test. Calculators can be used for any problem on the test, though calculators may be more harm than help for some questions.

Note: Unless otherwise stated on the test, you should assume the following:

1. Figures accompanying questions are not drawn to scale.
2. Geometric figures exist in a plane.
3. When given in a question, "line" refers to a straight line.
4. When given in a question, "average" refers to the arithmetic mean.

1. If $\frac{x+28}{7} = 8$, then what is the value of x?

   A. 84
   B. 56
   C. 52
   D. 28
   E. 2

2. A classroom contains 31 chairs, some of which have arms and some of which do not. If the room contains 5 more armchairs than chairs without arms, how many armchairs does it contain?

   F. 10
   G. 13
   H. 16
   J. 18
   K. 21

On the ACT Math Test, you'll get a question followed by five answer choices. One choice is correct; the other four are incorrect. Some incorrect choices will be *distractors*, or wrong choices that look temptingly correct. Math distractors tend to either repeat numbers from the problem or give a number you derive along the way to the right answer choice.

The first question is a *basic problem*. You won't see any complicated wording or context in these problems. They simply present you with a math problem in a no-frills fashion. In our sample question, you're asked to solve for x, so you'd set up an algebraic equation, then solve. Multiplying each side by 7 eliminates the fraction, yielding a simpler equation, which, in turn, gives $x = 28$, or **D**.

The second question is a *word problem*. As the name implies, word problems use words to describe a math problem. They're a little more complicated than basic problems because you have to sort through the words to find the math. Once you do, though, you have a basic problem on your hands. The correct answer here is **J**.

The rest of the directions are straightforward: Read the question, do the math, pick the right answer, don't overrely on the calculator. Math questions will always appear on the left side of the page, with the right side reserved for "your figuring." We'll discuss this empty space and what you should do with it in the Essential Strategies section of this Intensive. We'll also talk more about when to use your calculator and, most important, how to solve the problems.

ESSENTIAL CONCEPTS

Later in this Intensive we'll present a step method that you should employ on every math question you face. However, different problems call for different approaches, so one of the steps, "Plan the Attack," is open-ended and calls for you to choose the most effective approach to the problem at hand. So before we get to the step method itself, we'll first demonstrate a standard approach to ACT Math, as well as a few alternative approaches that may come in handy in particular situations. Therefore, we'll cover the following here:

1. Standard Applications of Math Concepts
2. Alternative Approaches for Special Cases

Essential Concept #1: Standard Applications of Math Concepts

Some questions require nothing more than straightforward applications of the algebra or geometry concepts you learned in junior high or high school. This doesn't necessarily mean that such questions will be easy. Some of the concepts themselves can be complex, and the test makers occasionally complicate matters by sprinkling traps among the choices.

Easier questions often require the application of a single concept, whereas harder questions may involve multiple concepts. Some may even require you to draw your own diagram when none is given. Regardless of the difficulty level, the standard application approach is the same: Scope out the situation, decide on what concept or concepts are being tested, and then use what you know about those concepts to answer the question before looking at the choices. If you've done your work well, the answer you get will be among the choices in the booklet, and you'll bubble it in and move on.

Let's look at a few examples spanning various difficulty levels. We'll work through single-concept questions based on one particular math concept and multiple-concept questions that require you to make use of many bits of math knowledge to arrive at the answer.

SINGLE-CONCEPT QUESTIONS

Here's an example of the simplest kind of math question you'll see:

3. What is the value of x if $3x - 27 = 33$?
   A. 2
   B. 11
   C. 20
   D. 27
   E. 35

The math concept in play in this basic problem is **equations with one variable**[*], something you likely remember from algebra class. There's nothing to do here but apply the concept: First, isolate the variable by adding 27 to both sides to get $3x = 60$, and then divide both sides by 3 to get $x = 20$, **C**. No doubt the test makers include 2 among the answer choices to trap people who accidentally *subtracted* 27 from the right side, yielding $3x = 6$ and $x = 2$. **B**, 11, is what you get if you divide one number in the problem (33) by another (3), and 27, **D**, appears in the problem itself. Assuming you didn't fall for any of these traps, there's not much to it: Just apply a single, fairly basic concept directly to the problem to pick up the point.

Not all single-concept questions are necessarily so straightforward, however, especially as you get on in the section. Try this word problem on for size:

---

[*]Again, if this or any other math concept trips you up, go online to **www.sparknotes. com/math/primer** and look it up on our math primer. Every math concept you need to know is covered.

4. At a local golf club, 75 members attend weekday lessons, 12 members attend weekend lessons, and 4 members attend both weekday and weekend lessons. If 10 members of the organization do not attend any lessons, how many members are in the club?

    F. 65
    G. 75
    H. 82
    J. 93
    K. 101

There's only one concept in play, but if you don't know it, you're in for a very tough time. You need the formula for **group problems with two groups: group 1 + group 2 – both + neither = total**. If we let *group 1* be the 75 members who attend weekday lessons and let *group 2* be the 12 members who attend weekend lessons, we get: 75 + 12 – 4 + 10 = *total*. Solving for *total* gives 93, **J**. Notice how **G**, 75, is a number contained in the problem, while **K**, 101, is what you get if you mistakenly *add* 4 instead of *subtract* it.

MULTIPLE-CONCEPT QUESTIONS

Some questions require you to pull together two or more choice tidbits from your math arsenal. One of the most common examples of a multiple-concept question involves geometric formulas that generate equations that need to be solved arithmetically and/or algebraically. Here's an example:

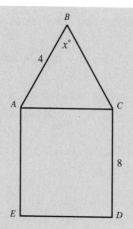

6. If $AB = BC$ and $x = 60$, what is the length of CE in rectangle $ACDE$?

F. 4
G. $4\sqrt{5}$
H. $5\sqrt{2}$
J. 8
K. 12

This question is a bit more involved than a typical single-concept question because there are a number of geometry concepts you need to know and some genuine opportunities to slip up on the arithmetic end too. It's also what we call a "mish-mash problem" because it involves several shapes: three triangles and a rectangle. If you don't know the special and exciting properties of these geometric figures, go online to the math primer. If you do know, you'll be able to at least formulate the correct equation for line EC, but then you *still* have to crunch the numbers to solve it. Let's see what a solid effort on this question might look like.

First, you're best off redrawing the diagram because you wouldn't want to keep all the information you're going to add to it in your head. If AB and BC are equal, $\angle BAC$ and $\angle BCA$ must be equal because **the angles** in a triangle opposite from equal sides are equal (concept 1). So the third angle labeled x equals 60°, ∠BAC and ∠BCA together must total 120° **because the three angles of a triangle add up to 180°** (concept 2). We determined that ∠BAC and ∠BCA are equal, so they both must be 60°. Notice anything now? **A triangle with three equal angles is an equilateral triangle** (concept 3). Because **all three sides in an equilateral triangle are equal** (concept 4), $AB = BC = AC = 4$. Because $ACDE$ is a rectangle, and **opposite sides of a rectangle are equal** (concept 5), $AC = ED = 4$. By now your sketch should look like this:

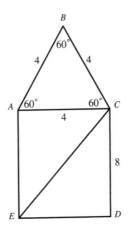

Now that we have two sides of right triangle ECD, we have everything we need to figure out the length of EC, thanks to the **Pythagorean theorem**: $x^2 + y^2 = z^2$ where x and y are the sides and z is the hypotenuse (concept 6). Substituting 4 and 8 as the sides and EC as the hypotenuse gives us this:

$$(EC)^2 = 4^2 + 8^2 =$$

For convenience, we'll denote all of the ensuing **arithmetic**, including **simplifying the radical**, as concept 7:

$$(EC)^2 = 4^2 + 8^2$$
$$(EC)^2 = 16 + 64$$
$$(EC)^2 = 80$$
$$EC = \sqrt{80}$$
$$EC = \sqrt{16}\sqrt{5}$$
$$EC = 4\sqrt{5}$$

Voila!—**G** is correct. Check out the traps: 4, **F**, is a number calculated along the way; 8, **J**, is a number given in the problem; and 12, **K**, is what you get if you add the two known sides of triangle *ECD* together.

Notice that no fewer than *seven* math concepts made their way into this problem—none of them particularly earth-shattering or treacherous, mind you, but still adding up to a medium-level challenge with plenty of potential pitfalls.

Essential Concept #2: Alternative Approaches for Special Cases

The standard "do question, look for answer" approach is all well and good, but some questions call out for alternative approaches. When the question contains variables in the answer choices, *making up numbers* and *substituting* them into the problem is often very effective. Conversely, when the answer choices contain actual numbers, you may benefit from simply plugging them back in to the given situation to see which one works, instead of hacking through some difficult operations or algebra. This is called *working backward*. Let's take a look at each of these approaches, one by one.

MAKING UP NUMBERS

Which of the following problems would you rather be faced with on test day?

- **Question 1:** If x apples cost y cents, how much will z apples cost in dollars?
- **Question 2:** If 5 apples cost 50 cents, how much will 10 apples cost in dollars?

If you're like most people, question 2 looks much easier, and you probably wouldn't have much trouble solving it: If you double the number of apples, you double the number of cents. One hundred cents equals one dollar. Done.

The difference between question 1 and question 2 is simple. We replaced the variables in question 1 with some made-up numbers, thus creating the easier question 2. So if you see x, y, m, n, or any other variables in both the question and the answer choices, consider avoiding complicated algebra by making up numbers and inserting them into the problem. You don't want to just make up any old numbers, however. You want numbers that will simplify the problem.

Use the following guidelines:

- **Pick easy numbers.** Although you could choose 582.97 as a value, you definitely wouldn't be making the problem any easier. Stick to relatively small, whole numbers whenever possible.

- **Avoid 0, 1, and any numbers used in the problem.** The numbers 0 and 1 have unique properties that may skew the results when used for this technique, so don't substitute either of those into the problem. Also, because the test makers sometimes use numbers from the question to construct distractors, you may get yourself into trouble by selecting those as well. If, for example, the problem contains the expression $3a + 5$, don't use 3 or 5. You shouldn't have any trouble avoiding the few numbers used in the question itself, just for good measure.

- **Choose different numbers for different variables.** For example, if the problem contains the variables m and n, you wouldn't want to choose 2 for both. Instead, you might choose 2 for m and 3 for n.

- **Pay attention to units.** If a problem involves a change in units (such as minutes to hours, pennies to dollars, feet to yards, and so on), choose a number that works well for both units. For example, 120 would be a good choice for a variable representing minutes, because 120 minutes is easily converted into 2 hours.

- **Obey the rules of the problem.** Occasionally, the problem may include specific requirements for variables. For example, if the problem says that x must be negative, you can't make up a positive value for x.

- **Save dependent variables for last.** If the value of one variable is determined by the value of one or more other variables, make up numbers for those other variables first. That will automatically determine the value of the variable that depends on the value of the others. For example, if the problem states that $a = b + c$, a is dependent on b and c. Choose values for b and c first, and the value of a will then simply emerge as the sum of b and c.

An actual number will emerge when you work out the problem with the numbers you've selected. All you need to do then is check which answer choice contains an expression that yields the same value when you make the same substitutions. This will make more sense in the context of an example, so let's work through a word problem together.

7. A gear makes r rotations in m minutes. If it rotates at a constant speed, how many rotations will the gear make in h hours?

A. $\dfrac{60r}{m}$

B. $\dfrac{60rh}{m}$

C. $\dfrac{60rm}{h}$

D. $\dfrac{rh}{m}$

E. $\dfrac{mrh}{60}$

Sure, you could crunch through this algebraically, and if that floats your boat, great. However, if you're among those who get a headache from just looking at questions like this, making up numbers may be just the way to go. Here's how.

The variables in this problem are r, m, and h. We can make up whatever values we'd like for these, as long as the values we choose make it easy to work the problem. For r, the number of rotations, let's choose something small, like 3. For m, the number of minutes, we should choose a value that will make it easy to convert to hours: 120 works well because 120 minutes is the same as 2 hours. Finally, for h, we should choose something small again.

Remember that we need to choose a different value for each variable, so let's use 4. Now that we have our numbers, simply plug them into the situation:

A gear makes **3** rotations in **120** minutes. If it rotates at a constant speed, how many rotations will the gear make in **4** hours?

Okay, much better—that's something we can sink our teeth into. 120 minutes is the same as 2 hours, during which time the gear rotates 3 times. If it rotates 3 times in 2 hours, how many times will it rotate in 4 hours? That's just twice as much time, so it will make twice as many rotations: $2 \times 3 = 6$, and so 6 is what we get when we substitute our values into the problem. Now we have to find the answer choice that's equal to 6 when the same values are substituted for its variables. Just work your way down the list, using 3 for r, 120 for m, and 4 for h:

A: $\dfrac{60r}{m} = \dfrac{(60)(3)}{120} = \dfrac{180}{20} = \dfrac{3}{2}$: That's not 6, the answer we seek, so move on.

B: $\dfrac{60rh}{m} = \dfrac{(60)(3)(4)}{120} = \dfrac{720}{120} = 6$: Yup—this is exactly what we're looking

for, so **B** is correct. If you're sure of your work, there's no need to even continue with the choices; you'd just pick **B** and move on to the next question. For practice, though, let's see how the other three pan out:

C: $\dfrac{60rm}{h} = \dfrac{(60)(3)(120)}{4} = 5,400$: Way too big.

D: $\dfrac{rh}{m} = \dfrac{(3)(4)}{120} = \dfrac{1}{10}$: Way too small.

E: $\dfrac{mrh}{60} = \dfrac{(120)(3)(4)}{60} = 24$: Four times bigger than what we're after.

Just what we thought: **B** is the only choice that matches the number we derived from our made-up numbers, so **B** gets the point.

You'll get more practice with this strategy as we go forward. Let's now move on to our other specialty technique, an exercise in role reversal that we call . . .

WORKING BACKWARD

When the question includes an equation (or a word problem that can be translated into an equation), and the answer choices contain relatively simple numbers, then it may be possible to plug the choices back in to the equation to see which one works.

Working backward from the choices may help you avoid setting up or solving complicated equations and can save you time as well because of a neat wrinkle of this technique: The choices in math questions are usually written in either ascending or descending order, so you can start with the middle choice, **C** or **H**, depending on whether the question is odd or even, and either get the answer immediately or at least eliminate three choices for the price of one. Here's how.

Let's say the answer choices are in ascending order. If you start by plugging in **C** (or **H**), then even if that choice doesn't work, you can use the outcome to determine whether you need to plug in a smaller or larger number. If you need a smaller number, then **D** (or **J**) and **E** (or **K**) are out of the question, and you can go right to **A** (or **F**) or **B** (or **G**). If instead you need a larger number, chop the first two choices and try the last two choices. Notice another nice feature: When you plug in for the second time, that choice will either work or leave only one choice standing. If you follow this alternative approach, you shouldn't ever have to check more than two choices.

As always, math strategies make the most sense in the context of examples, so we'll demonstrate using a question from the X-ray.

---

2. A classroom contains 31 chairs, some of which have arms and some of which do not. If the room contains 5 more armchairs than chairs without arms, how many armchairs does it contain?

   F. 10
   G. 13
   H. 16
   J. 18
   K. 21

Now if you happen to be an algebra whiz, you'd go ahead and use the information to set up a pair of *simultaneous equations* to solve this word problem. However, you may find it easier to work backward instead. The choices are in ascending order, so we'll start with the middle one and pretend it's correct. If it really *is* correct, then plugging it into the problem's scenario will cause all the numbers to work out, so let's see if it does.

The question is looking for the number of armchairs, which for the moment we're assuming to be 16. We can bounce that number off the information in the beginning of the second sentence (5 more armchairs than chairs without arms) to determine that with 16 armchairs, there would have to be 11 chairs without arms. Now all we have to do is check whether this scenario matches the information in the first sentence. Would that give us 31 chairs total? Nope: 16 + 11 = 27, so the numbers don't jibe. That tells us three things: **H** isn't correct, **G** isn't correct, and **F** isn't correct. We can knock out **F** and **G** along with **H** because they're both *smaller* than **H**, and if the number in **H** isn't big enough to get us to our required 31 chairs, **F** and **G** ain't gonna cut it either.

Now let's try **J**—if it works, it's correct, and if it doesn't, we can select **K** without even trying it out: 18 armchairs means $18 - 5 = 13$ chairs without arms, and $18 + 13 = 31$ chairs total. That matches the information in the question, so **J** is correct. Note that you could have worked the numbers the other way: If there are 31 chairs total, and we assume there are 18 armchairs, then there would have to be 13 chairs without arms. That matches the information in the second sentence that requires 5 more armchairs than ones without arms. Either way you slice it, the number 18 fits the bill when plugged back into the situation, and we didn't have to bother with creating and solving simultaneous equations.

Standard Applications vs. Alternative Approaches

We want to stress that neither an alternative approach nor the standard approach is necessarily better. There are faster and slower ways, depending on your strengths in math. Of course, it always benefits you to use the faster way if you can, but the most important thing is getting the question right.

Trying to solve problems using the standard approach is conceptually demanding but can take less time. Working backward or making up numbers makes questions easier to tackle but will likely take more time. Use your judgment as to when to work backward. If there are numbers in the answer choices, then consider it, but don't do it if the numbers are unwieldy, such as complex fractions. One of the skills that the best math test takers possess is the ability to determine the most effective way to work through the problems. We've shown you standard approaches and a few powerful alternatives. In the next section, we'll review some Essential Strategies, including the general step method, you'll use on all ACT Math questions.

ESSENTIAL STRATEGIES

Here are the math strategies to keep in mind on test day:

- Draw Pictures
- Use Your Calculator Wisely
- Avoid Partial Answers
- Use the Math Test Step Method

Draw Pictures

On the right-hand side of every Math Test page, you will find a column with the header "DO YOUR FIGURING HERE." You can use this space to write formulas, graphs, drawings of triangles, or whatever else you want. This space can be particularly useful for drawing figures that are not provided with the question. If you have a hard time visualizing shapes in your head, draw them in the test booklet. If a question asks you about a polygon but doesn't provide a figure, you can draw one of your own if it will help you solve the problem.

While writing out your answers or drawing figures can be extremely helpful, it can also be time consuming. No one will see your test booklet, so don't worry about trying to be neat or artistic. Do just as much writing or drawing as you need to do in order to get the question right: no more, no less.

Use Your Calculator Wisely

Just because you are permitted to use your calculator doesn't mean that you should go calculator crazy. Every question on the ACT can be solved without using a calculator, so you never need to start pushing buttons. Calculators can certainly be helpful on some problems, but on others using a calculator might actually take more time than working out the problems by hand.

When you use your calculator on the test, it should be because you have thought about the question, have a good sense of how to proceed, and see how your calculator can help you. Keep the following "dos and don'ts" in mind:

- **Do** use your calculator for any brute-force tasks, such as dealing with decimals.
- **Don't** use your calculator if you have to deal with a long string of numbers. Instead, look for a way to cancel out some of the terms and simplify. A way will usually exist.
- **Don't** use your calculator on fraction problems or on algebra questions with variables.
- **Do** know how to use your calculator before the test. Be comfortable and familiar with it so you don't waste time fiddling with buttons during the test. This is particularly true of graphing calculators.

Above all else, remember: Your calculator is a tool. You wouldn't wildly swing a hammer around, but some students seem to think they can just whip out their calculator and it will magically solve their problems. Those students seldom do well on ACT Math.

Avoid Partial Answers

For problems that have more than one step, a partial answer is the answer to one of the steps of the problem, but not to the whole problem. For example:

8. On Monday, a bus carries 10 girls and 5 boys. On Tuesday, it carries 5 girls and 6 boys. What is the average number of girls and boys on the bus over the period of Monday and Tuesday?

F. 0
G. 11
H. 13
J. 15
K. 26

The correct answer to this question is **H**, 13 girls and boys, but you may have liked **G**, **J**, or **K**, which are all partial answers to this problem (**F** is just silly). Here's why you might have chosen **G**, **J**, or **K**: **G** is the total number of passengers on the Tuesday bus, **J** is the total number of passengers on the Monday bus, and **K** is the total number of passengers riding for both days. You have to calculate each one of these numbers to get the final answer (**K** divided by the number of days, 2). At any point during those calculations, you may have looked down and seen that a number you had calculated matched a number in the answer choices. Then you may have assumed you found the right answer. But, no, you didn't.

Partial answers love to prey upon eager test takers who are in a hurry to get the right answer. Instead of paying careful attention to the question, these test takers get a number, see it in the answer choices, and immediately identify it as the correct answer. ACT knows about all these eager, jumpy test takers and deliberately plants partial answers throughout the Math Test.

On word problems, the last sentence of the problem usually tells you what the question is looking for. Consider rereading this last sentence once you've formulated your answer to make sure you did what the question asked.

Use the Math Test Step Method

Here's the method to use on every math question you'll see on test day:

Step 1: Get the Specs.

Step 2: Plan the Attack.

Step 3: Mine the Math.

Step 4: Power Through.

Before we tackle some sample problems, let's see how the steps work:

Step 1: Get the Specs. Step 1 puts you in the right frame of mind to successfully work through a math question. The main specifications that should interest you include the following:

- What kind of math problem is it? A basic problem or a word problem? Word problems tend to take more time because you have to translate the words into math.
- What general subject area—algebra, geometry, or trigonometry—is being tested?

Step 2: Plan the Attack. In Step 2, you'll determine your approach—that is, whether you'll use the standard approach and then search the choices for the answer you get, or whether it's better to make up numbers or work backward. Use the information you discovered in Step 1 to help you decide how to proceed.

Step 3: Mine the Math. With a solid plan in mind, you'll then dig through your math knowledge to figure out what you need to use to solve the problem. If the question concerns a right triangle, for example, then the Pythagorean theorem and rules for the length of the sides of right triangles should pop into your head. If you're up against exponents, an arithmetic mean situation, or a quadratic equation, then you'd pull concepts related to those topics from your reservoir of math knowledge. Don't think you have to gather every single concept you'll need at this stage; some necessary concepts will emerge as you proceed through the problem in Step 4. In Step 3, simply dig out the math you need to get started.

Step 4: Power Through. With the relevant math and a plan firmly in mind, you'll now be able to power through the question. "Power Through," however, doesn't necessarily imply using brute force, for in many cases, clever or elegant solutions may be possible. How you do the work will depend on the method you choose in Step 2, and in many cases the standard approach works fine. But in other cases you may settle on one of the alternative approaches. Either way, Step 4 is the time to solve the problem.

Let's work through some examples.

---

5. If the average of 13, 6, 9, x, and y is 12, what is the average of $x + y$?

   A. 6

   B. 9

   C. 12

   D. 16

   E. 32

Step 1: Get the Specs. This is a basic algebra problem.

Step 2: Plan the Attack. We have a set of five items, two of which are variables. We need to find the **average** of the two variables. Let's use the standard application of math concepts.

Step 3: Mine the Math. Based on our Step 2 plan, we know we need the **mean/average equation**:

$$\text{mean} = \frac{\text{sum of all items}}{\text{number of items}}$$

Step 4: Power Through. Now that we know what to do, it's time to do the math. The average of the five items is 12, $12 = \left(\frac{\text{sum}}{5}\right)$. So the sum is 60. If the sum is 60, and three of the items are 13, 6, and 9, then the sum of the last two must be $60 - (13 + 6 + 9)$, or 32.

We're not quite done yet. 32 looks pretty good, and it's one of the answer choices, but *it's not what the item asked for*. To find their average, divide 32 by 2 to get 16.

The correct answer is **D**, 16.

Here's another example:

9. If $5x + 18 = 63$, what is the value of x?

   A. 5
   B. 9
   C. 13
   D. 17
   E. 40

Step 1: Get the Specs. This question gives us an algebraic equation, then asks us to figure out the value of the variable x. It's as basic a problem as basic problems can be.

Step 2: Plan the Attack. There are two ways to find x. We could work through the equation, manipulating the numbers as necessary until we isolate x. Or we could work backward, plugging the values into the equation. That option sounds good.

Step 3: Mine the Math. We're working backward and plugging in the values, so there's no math to mine. We can head straight to Step 4.

Step 4: Power Through. Let's solve this bad boy. Start with **C**: $5(13) + 18 = 65 + 18 = 83$. That's too high, so **C** is too big. **D** and **E** are even bigger, so they must also be wrong. That leaves **A** and **B**.

We have to try only one of them to get the answer. Let's say we pick **A**: $5(5) + 18 = 25 + 18 = 43$. That's too low, so **A** is too small. That leaves **B**, which is correct. And sure enough: $5(9) + 18 = 45 + 18 = 63$.

---

10. What is 0.5 percent of 55?

    F. .275
    G. 2.75
    H. 27.5
    J. 50
    K. 110

Step 1: Get the Specs. Not much to it, is there? It's a basic problem that draws on our understanding of pre-algebra. Nothing too crazy.

Step 2: Plan the Attack. A straightforward approach is the way to go. We'll dig out the math concept we need and use it to do the math.

Step 3: Mine the Math. Adding the word percent to a number means taking that number two places to the left when converting it to a decimal. For example, 20 percent = 0.2. In this example, 0.5 percent = 0.005. The other thing you need to know is that the word *of* means "multiplication"; whenever we take a certain percent of something, we multiply the figures.

Step 4: Power Through. Let's do the math: .005 × 55 = 0.275, so you'd choose **F** and move on. Maybe you just multiplied it out by hand or instead used approximations to get into the ballpark. Here's one way you can work through it without actually multiplying: 10 percent of 55 is 5.5, so to get 1 percent of 55, we just move the decimal place back one more place, giving us 0.55. Now, 0.5 percent is half of 1 percent, so we have to divide 0.55 by 2, which gives us 0.275.

Though the question is a straightforward test of your arithmetic knowledge, there are still a few concepts you need to know, some steps you need to perform, and some traps that could potentially trip you up.

---

11. A clothes designer must choose 3 of 10 possible fabrics for a single outfit. What is the total number of different outfits that the designer can create given this requirement?

    A. 70
    B. 120
    C. 130
    D. 150
    E. 300

Step 1: Get the Specs. The lingo in this pre-algebraic word problem should alert you to what you're up against—*choose 3 of 10 possible fabrics* indicates that this is either a **permutation** or **combination problem**. The question is, which is it? We'll settle that matter in Step 3 when we dig down into our stockpile of useful math information.

Step 2: Plan the Attack. Permutation and combination problems require little more than crunching through a formula, so our plan will be to take a standard approach, work through the formula, and solve. Of course, you have to *know* the formula to use, so the battle in this one is pretty much won or lost in Step 3.

Step 3: Mine the Math. The key to determining whether to use the combination or permutation formula is figuring out whether order is significant. In a race or ranking, clearly order matters. But in an *outfit*? Does anyone look at an outfit and say, "Hey, that outfit has some wool, and after that it has some polyester"? No, of course not. If it has both, it has both—it doesn't contain one before the other. Order is significant in permutations but not in combinations, so we're in combination territory. The combination formula is:

$$_nC_r = \frac{n!}{(n-r)!\,r!}$$

where unordered subgroups of size r are selected from a set of size n. A **factorial (!) following a number represents the product of all the numbers up to and including that number.**

Step 4: Power Through. If you know what permutations and combinations are, how to determine which to use in which circumstances, and the formulas and how to solve them, then the rest is definitely doable. As we said above, the battle in this question takes place primarily in Step 3. If you know all the concepts discussed in the previous step, the rest is little more than number crunching. Here goes:

$$_{10}C_3 = \frac{10!}{(10-3)!3!}$$

$$= \frac{10!}{7!3!}$$

$$= \frac{10 \times 9 \times 8 \times 7!}{7!3!}$$

$$= \frac{10 \times 9 \times 8}{3 \times 2 \times 1} = \frac{720}{6} = 120$$

The answer is 120, or **B**. Let's try one last problem.

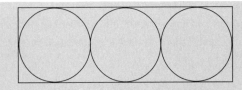

12. If the area of each of the three identical circles inscribed in the rectangle above is 25π, what is the perimeter of the rectangle?

   F. 30
   G. 40
   H. 60
   J. 75
   K. 80

This one's a toughie. We'll cut it down to size using our step method:

Step 1: Get the Specs. A nifty little circle/rectangle picture comes along with this basic geometry question, so we may need to employ some creative visualization to see how a part of one shape tells us what we need to know about the other. This is definitely a multiple-concept question because we need to draw on our knowledge of multiple geometric shapes.

Step 2: Plan the Attack. There's no alternative approach to use here, so we'll just apply what we know about circles and rectangles to get the information we need to solve the problem.

Step 3: Mine the Math. Here are the geometry math concepts we'll need: **The area of a circle = πr^2, where r is the radius. The diameter of a circle = twice its radius, $2r$. The perimeter of a rectangle = the sum of its sides.**

Step 4: Power Through. Did you see the relationship between the three circles and the rectangle's perimeter? The width of the rectangle is equal to the diameter of each circle, while the length of the rectangle equals the diameter of the first circle + the diameter of the second circle + the diameter of the third circle. So if we find the diameter of the circles (all equal because the circles are identical), then we can find the rectangle's perimeter.

Start with what we know: The area of each circle is 25π. Plugging that into our area formula, we get:

$$\text{area} = \pi r^2$$
$$25\pi = \pi r^2$$
$$25 = r^2$$
$$r = 5$$

If the radius of each circle is 5, then the diameter is 10. The width of the rectangle is therefore 10, and its length is $10 + 10 + 10 = 30$. The rectangle therefore has two sides of width 10 and two sides of length 30. The perimeter is therefore $10 + 10 + 30 + 30 = 80$, or **K**.

PRACTICE SET

Several multiple-choice questions follow. As always, remember the strategies and step method. Don't forget to check out the explanations to every question.

1. Marissa has a basket of red, yellow, and pink roses in a ratio of 6:3:2. The basket contains a total of 44 roses. How many pink roses are in the basket?

    A. 2
    B. 6
    C. 8
    D. 12
    E. 14

2. In the right triangle shown below, if $\sin\theta = \dfrac{4}{13}$ then $\cos\theta = ?$

    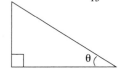

    F. $\dfrac{4}{3\sqrt{17}}$

    G. $\dfrac{4}{3}$

    H. $\dfrac{13}{3\sqrt{17}}$

    J. $\dfrac{3\sqrt{17}}{13}$

    K. $\dfrac{\sqrt{13}}{4}$

3. In the standard (x,y) coordinate plane, what is the slope of the line given by the equation $2x - 7y = 12$?

   A. $-\dfrac{2}{7}$

   B. -2

   C. $\dfrac{2}{7}$

   D. $\dfrac{7}{2}$

   E. 7

4. A package of 12 pencils is priced at $1.20 now. If the pencils go on sale for 25% off the current price, what will be the sale price of the package?

   F. $0.60
   G. $0.70
   H. $0.80
   J. $0.90
   K. $1.00

5. What are the measures of the two angles shown in the figure below?

   A. 36°, 54°
   B. 18°, 72°
   C. 36°, 144°
   D. 27°, 63°
   E. 72°, 108°

6. When $x = \dfrac{1}{3}$, what is the value of $\dfrac{9x - 2}{x}$?

F. −30

G. −3

H. $-\dfrac{1}{3}$

J. 1

K. 3

7. Newbreak Coffee Company baristas mix Arabian Mocha Java and Colombian coffees together to make the store's Sunrise Blend. Three pounds of Arabian Mocha Java plus five pounds of Colombian cost $73. Four pounds of Arabian Mocha Java plus eight pounds of Colombian cost $110. Let a = price per pound of Arabian Mocha Java and c = price per pound of Colombian. What is the price per pound (a, c) of the two types of coffee?

A. $9.75, $10.50
B. $8.50, $9.50
C. $12.50, $10.50
D. $10.50, $9.75
E. $9.50, $8.50

8. If b blocks of cement cost d dollars, how many cents will x blocks of cement cost at the same rate?

F. $\dfrac{xd}{b}$

G. $100xbd$

H. $\dfrac{xbd}{10}$

J. $100\dfrac{xd}{b}$

K. $100\dfrac{xb}{d}$

9. The length *a* of the ship *Amazon Queen* is 30 feet more than four-fifths the length *w* of the *Arctic Wolf*. Which of the following expresses the relationship between *a* and *w*?

A. $a = \frac{4}{5}w - 30$

B. $w = \frac{4}{5}a + 30$

C. $w = \frac{4}{5}w - 30$

D. $a = \frac{4}{5}w + 30$

E. $a + 30 = \frac{4}{5}w + 30$

10. In the standard (*x,y*) coordinate plane, the slope, *m*, of a line that goes through the point (0,0) is –1. What is the relationship between the *x*- and *y*-coordinates of each point on the line?

F. The *x*-coordinate is twice the *y*-coordinate.

G. The *x*-coordinate is one-half the *y*-coordinate.

H. The *x*- and *y*-coordinates are the same number.

J. The *y*-coordinate is the negative of the *x*-coordinate.

K. The *y*-coordinate is one-half the *x*-coordinate.

11. Delivery costs for Ocean Beach Hardware increased by 45% because the store moved further away from the warehouse. If it cost Ocean Beach Hardware $90 to ship tools before the store moved, how much would it cost to ship the same tools after the move?

A. $49.50

B. $62.75

C. $130.50

D. $165.25

E. $180.00

12. Three distinct lines, all contained in a plane, intersect each of the other two lines in exactly one point per line. How many distinct regions are formed by the three lines?

    F. 3
    G. 4
    H. 5
    J. 6
    K. 7

13. Which of the following are the solutions of $6x^2 - 11x - 10 = 0$?

    A. $-\dfrac{2}{3}, \dfrac{5}{2}$

    B. $\dfrac{5}{3}, -1$

    C. $-\dfrac{1}{3}, 5$

    D. $-\dfrac{5}{3}, 1$

    E. $-\dfrac{5}{2}, \dfrac{2}{3}$

14. The daily totals of dinner customers served at the Little Chef restaurant last Tuesday through Sunday were 232, 263, 298, 472, 451, and 372. What was the average number of lunch customers served each day?

    F. 2,088
    G. 872
    H. 567
    J. 451
    K. 348

15. In $\triangle ABC$ shown below, the measure of $\overline{AC}$ is 10 inches and $\overline{AB}$ is $5\sqrt{13}$ inches. What is the measure of $\overline{BC}$ in inches?

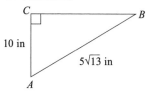

A. 12

B. 15

C. $\sqrt{325}$

D. 10

E. $5\sqrt{15}$

16. A circular tile sundial with a diameter of 15 meters is placed flat on the ground within the perimeter of a 30 meter by 60 meter rectangular lawn. What is the approximate area of the lawn that is not covered by the sundial?

F. 75

G. 1,093

H. 1,575

J. 1,623

K. 1,800

17. A coin flipped a number of times landed on heads y more times than twice the number of times it landed on tails. If h is the number of times the coin landed on heads, how many times was the coin flipped, expressed in terms of h and y?

A. $h + y$

B. $y + \dfrac{h}{2}$

C. $\dfrac{h - y}{2}$

D. $\dfrac{3y - h}{3}$

E. $\dfrac{3h - y}{2}$

18. Which of the following is the volume of the rectangular solid shown below?

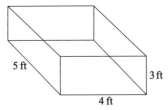

F. 12
G. 20
H. 23
J. 50
K. 60

19. If $0° \leq \theta° \leq 90°$ and $4 \cos^2 \theta° - 3 = 0$ then $\theta = ?$

A. 0°
B. 30°
C. 45°
D. 60°
E. 90°

20. Which of the following is the factorization of the binomial $x^2 - 4^2$?

F. $x(x + 2x + 2)$
G. $(x - 4)^2$
H. $(x + 4)(x + 2)$
J. $(x - 4)(x + 4)$
K. $(x + 4)^2$

Guided Explanations

1. C

This word problem lets you know that for every 6 red roses, you also have 3 yellow and 2 pink roses. This means that out of every 11 roses, 2 of them will be pink. Set up a proportion, and Power Through:

$$\frac{2}{11} = \frac{x}{44}$$
$$88 = 11x$$
$$x = 8$$

2. J

This basic trig problem tells you that $\sin\theta = \frac{4}{13}$. We'll use the standard application of math concepts to solve. The sine of angle θ is the ratio of the side opposite θ and the hypotenuse. This means that the side opposite θ is 4, and the hypotenuse is 13. See the figure below.

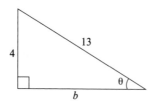

The cosine of angle θ is the ratio of the side adjacent to θ and the hypotenuse. To find $\cos\theta$, you must solve for the length of b using the Pythagorean theorem:

Pythagorean theorem	$c^2 = a^2 + b^2$
Substitute	$13^2 = 4^2 + b^2$
Simplify	$169 = 16 + b^2$
Subtract 16 from both sides	$153 = b^2$
Take the square root of both sides	$\sqrt{153} = b$
Factor	$\sqrt{9 \cdot 17} = b$
Simplify	$3\sqrt{17} = b$

In this problem, the side adjacent to θ is $3\sqrt{17}$ and the hypotenuse is 13, so $\cos\theta = \dfrac{3\sqrt{17}}{13}$.

3. C

Write the equation in **slope-intercept form** by solving for y. Once you solve for y, the coefficient on the x term is the slope of the line.

	$2x - 7y = 12$
Subtract $2x$ from each side	$-2x \qquad -2x$
Simplify	$-7y = -2x + 12$
Divide each term by -7	$y = \dfrac{2}{7}x - \dfrac{12}{7}$

The coefficient on the x term is $\dfrac{2}{7}$, so the slope of the line is positive and you can eliminate the two negative choices, **A** and **B**. Because the coefficient on the x term represents the slope, m, the slope of the line is $\dfrac{2}{7}$, **C**.

4. J

A straightforward word problem. The sale price is $100\% - 25\% = 75\%$ of the current price. Change 75% to a decimal and multiply it by the current price: $(0.75)(\$1.20) = \$0.90$, which means **J** is the right answer.

5. A

The sum of the two angles must equal 90° because the x-axis and y-axis form sides of the angles. Add the two angles and solve for z:

$$3z + 2z = 90°$$
$$5z = 90°$$
$$z = 18$$

Find the measure of the two angles by substituting $z = 18°$ into the expression for each angle:

$$3z = 3(18°) = 54°$$
$$2z = 2(18°) = 36°$$

6. K

Substitute $\frac{1}{3}$ in place of the x in both places where it appears and simplify:

$$\frac{9\left(\frac{1}{3}\right) - 2}{\frac{1}{3}} = \frac{3 - 2}{\frac{1}{3}}$$
$$\frac{3 - 2}{\frac{1}{3}} = \frac{1}{\frac{1}{3}}$$
$$\frac{1}{\frac{1}{3}} = 3$$

The correct answer is **K**.

7. B

Write a **system of equations** to represent this word problem, where a = price per pound of Arabian Mocha Java, and c = price per pound of Colombian:

$$3a + 5c = \$73$$
$$4a + 8c + \$110$$

Solve the system by the elimination method. Multiply each term in the first equation by -4 and each term in the second equation by 3 and then add the equations together to eliminate the variable a:

$$(-4)3a + (-4)5c = (-4)\$73$$
$$(3)4a + (3)\,8c + (3)\,\$110$$

$$-12a - 20c = \$292$$
$$12a + 24c = \$330$$

$$4c = \$38$$
$$c = \$9.50$$

Substitute $\$9.50$ in place of c in the first equation to solve for a:

$$3a + 5(\$9.50) = \$73$$
$$3a + \$47.50) = \$73$$
$$3a = \$25.50$$
$$a = \$8.50$$

The solution is ($\$8.50$, $\$9.50$), which is **B**.

8. J

This is a tough word problem. We've got three variables in the question and some nasty looking combinations of them in the choices. The phrase *at the same rate* tells us that some sort of ratio is in play.

Questions with difficult algebraic expressions in the choices are good candidates for our "making up numbers" alternative approach, so that's just what we'll do: make up some numbers, see where they lead, and find the choice that matches the value we get.

It pays to remember that **the units of a problem must be kept consistent throughout**. Here, that's important because information is provided in terms of both dollars and cents, so you have to make sure to convert where appropriate. Also, **a ratio is a fraction**, and **if the same ratio applies to different scenarios, we can set those fractions equal to each other**.

As we Power Through, we'll use the easiest numbers we can think of, outside of 0 and 1 (which tend to wreak havoc in these kinds of problems). Letting $b = 2$, $d = 3$, and $x = 4$ gives the problem a much better real-world feel: "If 2 blocks of cement cost 3 dollars, how many cents will 4 blocks of cement cost at the same rate?" Let's set up a simple equivalency ratio and solve it first in dollars, and then convert to cents:

$$\frac{2 \text{ blocks}}{3 \text{ dollars}} = \frac{4 \text{ blocks}}{a \text{ dollars}}$$

You can solve the equation by cross-multiplying or by seeing that doubling the number of blocks from 2 to 4 results in doubling the number of dollars from 3 to 6. The question asks for the number of cents required, so we should now convert the 6 dollars to 600 cents. That's the value that emerges from the numbers we made up. Now all we have to do is see which of the choices comes out to 600 when we plug in 2 for b, 3 for d, and 4 for x. Let's try them:

F: $\dfrac{xd}{b} = \dfrac{4 \times 3}{2} = 6$: This one looks good only if you forget to convert dollars to cents. Otherwise, no-go.

G: $100xbd = 100 \times 4 \times 2 \times 3 = 2400$: Too big.

H: $\dfrac{xbd}{10} = \dfrac{4 \times 2 \times 3}{10} = 2.4$: *Too* small.

J: $100\dfrac{xd}{b} = 100 \times \dfrac{4 \times 3}{2} = 100 \times 6 = 600$: It works! Just for the record:

K: $100\dfrac{xb}{d} = 100\dfrac{4 \times 2}{3} = 100 \times \dfrac{8}{3} =$ not 600, whichever way you slice it.

9. D

Translate the word problem into a math equation: "The length of the ship *Amazon Queen*" is represented by *a*, and the word *is* means "=." The expression "30 feet more than" means you add 30 feet to whatever comes next. *Four-fifths* is written as the fraction $\dfrac{4}{5}$, *of* means "multiplication," and "the length of the *Arctic Wolf*" is represented by *w*. Put the terms together in a math equation:

$$a = \frac{4}{5}w + 30$$

10. J

A **slope** of –1 means that from the point (0,0) on the line, you can get to another point by moving down 1 (because of the negative sign) and over 1 to the right in the coordinate plane. The coordinates of this new point are (1,–1). If you go down 1 and over 1 to the right again, you are at the point (2,–2). Notice the relationship between the coordinates in each pair: The y-coordinate is the negative of the x-coordinate, which is **J**.

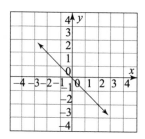

11. C

An increase of 45% means the new delivery cost is 100% + 45% = 145% of the current cost. Turn this percent into a decimal number and multiply by $90 to find the new delivery cost: (1.45)($90) = $130.50. This means that **C** is the right answer.

12. K

You are given the information that three lines intersect the other two lines in one point per line. This means the three lines form a triangle. This breaks the plane into seven distinct regions that are numbered in the diagram below, so the answer is **K**.

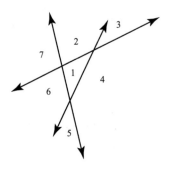

13. A

Look to see if you can divide out a common factor from each term. You can't, so set up two sets of parentheses with the factors of $6x^2$ as the first term in the parentheses and factors of -10 as the second term in the parentheses:

$$(3x - 5)(2x + 2)$$

Distribute using **FOIL,** an acronym that describes the order in which we multiply the terms of two binomials to get the correct product: **First + Outer + Inner + Last.** Then simplify to see if you get back to $6x^2 - 11x - 10$:

$$(3x - 5)(2x + 2) = 6x^2 - 4x - 10$$

You do not, so switch the -5 and $+2$ and try again:

$$(3x + 2)(2x - 5) = 6x^2 - 11x - 10$$

This time you get back to the original trinomial. Now set each factor equal to 0 and solve for x.

$$3x + 2 = 0 \qquad 2x - 5 = 0$$
$$3x = -2 \qquad 2x = 5$$
$$x = -\frac{2}{3} \qquad x = \frac{5}{2}$$

These solutions match **A**.

14. K

The **average** is found by adding up the numbers you are given (232, 263, 298, 472, 451, and 372) and dividing by the number of numbers you are given (6). Add: $232 + 263 + 298 + 472 + 451 + 372 = 2{,}088$. Divide: $2{,}088 \div 6 = 348$. This makes **K** the right answer.

15. B

Set up the **Pythagorean theorem**: $(\overline{AB})^2 = (\overline{AB})^2 + (\overline{BC})^2$. Substitute 10 for $\overline{AC}$ and $5\sqrt{13}$ for $\overline{AB}$ in the equation and solve for $\overline{BC}$:

	$(\overline{AB})^2 = (\overline{AB})^2 + (\overline{BC})^2$
Substitue	$(5\sqrt{13})^2 = 10^2 + (\overline{BC})^2$
Simplify	$325 = 100 + (\overline{BC})^2$
Subtract 100 from both sides	$225 = (\overline{BC})^2$
Take the square root of both sides	$15 = \overline{BC}$

16. J

Find the area of the rectangular lawn using the **area of a rectangle** formula ($A = lw$) and subtract the area of the circular sundial using the **area of a circle** formula ($A = \pi r^2$). Use 3.14159 for π, and diameter ÷ 2 for the radius:

$$A = lw - \pi r^2$$
$$A = (30 \text{ meters})(60 \text{ meters}) - 3.14159(15 \text{ meters} \div 2)^2$$
$$A = 1{,}800 \text{ meters}^2 - 3.14159(56.25 \text{ meters}^2)$$
$$A = 1{,}800 \text{ meters}^2 - 176.7 \text{ meters}^2$$
$$A = 1{,}623.3 \text{ meters}^2$$
$$A \approx 1{,}623 \text{ meters}^2$$

17. E

Word problems containing variables lend themselves naturally to algebraic solutions, so if you're comfortable with algebra, you could Power Through this one by setting up and solving some basic equations. Alternatively, the variables scattered across the answer choices suggest that this problem may also lend itself well to our making-up-numbers strategy, so you may have chosen that route instead. Tell you what—for practice, we'll do both.

For the algebraic approach, you'll need to draw on your knowledge of constructing and solving multiple equations. For both approaches, you'll need to correctly translate the English into math.

Algebra Style. First, the English-to-math translation: If we designate tails as t, then *twice the number of times it landed on tails* is $2t$. Y more times than *twice the number of times it landed on tails* is therefore $2t + y$. Using h for heads as instructed, our equation becomes $h = 2t + y$. The question is looking for the total number of flips, which is the number of heads plus the number of tails, or $h + t$. However, the question asks for the total expressed in terms of h and y. No problem—we can solve for t in terms of y in our first equation and substitute that into the equation representing the total:

$$h = 2t + y$$
$$2t = h - y$$
$$t = \frac{h - y}{2}$$

Now replace t with this new value in the total equation:

$$\text{total flips} = h + t$$
$$= h + \frac{h - y}{2}$$

Now some basic arithmetic is in order, making this a multiple-concept question. We can use the Magic X to simplify our equation to

$$\text{total flips} = \frac{2h + h - y}{2} \ \text{ or } \ \frac{3h - y}{2}, \text{ choice } \mathbf{E}.$$

Making Up Numbers. Okay, so what if all those equations in the previous solution look like Egyptian hieroglyphics to you? Then the "make up numbers" alternative approach is the way to go. We start the same way by translating the wording of the question into the expression $h = 2t + y$. Variable h is the dependent variable because its value is determined by the values of t and y, so when it comes to picking numbers, we'll want to save h for last. In this case, we'll only need to use our imagination for t and y, since h will follow from those. And remember to go with simple numbers—why make your life more difficult than it needs to be? $T = 2$ is friendly enough; a nice small number that's easy to double. $2t$ is 4, so if we set $y = 6$, then h will be an even 10, giving us:

$$t = 2$$
$$y = 6$$
$$h = 10$$

With all the variables set, we can focus on what the question is after. The total number of flips equals the number of heads plus the number of tails. In our imaginary world, that's 10 + 2 = 12. Now we simply need to determine which combination of h's and y's in the choices calculates to 12. Let's try them out.

A: $h + y = 10 + 6 = 16$: No good.

B: $y + \dfrac{h}{2} = 6 + 5 = 11$: Nope.

C: $\dfrac{h - y}{2} = \dfrac{4}{2} = 2$: Uh-uh.

D: $\dfrac{3y - h}{3} = \dfrac{8}{3}$: Not even close.

E: $\dfrac{3h - y}{2} = \dfrac{24}{2} = 12$: That's the one. **E** is correct, no matter which approach we take.

18. K

The volume of a rectangular solid is found by multiplying the length, width, and height:

$$V = lwh$$

Substitute 5 ft for length, 4 ft for width, and 3 ft for height into the formula and simplify:

$$V = lwh$$
$$V = (5 \text{ ft})(4 \text{ ft})(3 \text{ ft})$$
$$V = 60 \text{ ft}^3$$

19. B

This basic problem wants you to solve the identity for cos θ:

Given identity	$4\cos^2\theta - 3 = 0$
Add 3 to both sides	$4\cos^2\theta = 3$
Divide both sides by 4	$\cos^2\theta = \dfrac{3}{4}$
Take the square root of both sides	$\cos\theta = \dfrac{\sqrt{3}}{2}$

Find θ by taking the inverse cosine of $\dfrac{\sqrt{3}}{2}$: $\cos^{-1}\dfrac{\sqrt{3}}{2} = 30°$. Notice that the answer choices are in degrees, so be sure that your calculator is in degree mode before you take the inverse cosine. The correct answer is **B**.

20. J

This **binomial** is the difference of two squares. The formula for the difference of two squares is $a^2 - b^2 = (a - b)(a + b)$. In this problem, $a = x$ and $b = 4$. Substitute x for a and 4 for b in the formula and simplify:

$$a^2 - b^2 = (a - b)(a + b)$$
$$x^2 - 4^2 = (x - 4)(x + 4)$$

INTENSIVE 3

The Reading Test

Reading Test X-ray

Essential Concepts

Essential Strategies

The Big Five Question Types

Special Advice for Prose Fiction

Practice Set

THE ACT READING TEST CONSISTS OF 40 QUESTIONS spread out among four passages; it lasts for 35 minutes. Basically, you're given a passage, then asked 10 questions about what you've just read. You'll repeat this procedure four times in a very short span of time.

Unlike the English and Math Tests, the Reading Test evaluates a set of skills you've acquired rather than learned. As the test's name implies, these skills are your ability to read and comprehend different types of passages. We'll discuss the passages types and questions later in this Intensive. For now, let's start with an X-ray.

READING TEST X-RAY

Here's a sample passage with a few sample questions, similar to what you'll see on test day. We'll refer to this passage throughout the Essential Concepts section, and we'll work through the questions in the section on the Big Five Question Types.

DIRECTIONS: On this test, you will have 35 minutes to read four passages and answer 40 questions (ten questions on each passage). Each set of ten questions appears directly after the relevant passage. You should select the answer choice that best answers the question. There is no time limit for work on the individual passages, so you can move freely between the passages and refer to each as often as you'd like.

SOCIAL SCIENCE: This passage is adapted from Doris Stevens's *Jailed for Freedom* (1920).

"Where are the people?" This was Woodrow Wilson's first question as he arrived at the Union Station in Washington the day before his first inauguration to the Presidency in March, 1913.

"On the Avenue watching the suffragists parade," came the answer.

5 The suffrage issue was brought to his attention from then on until his final surrender. It lay entirely with him as to how long women would be obliged to remind him of this issue before he decided to take a hand.

"The people" were on the Avenue watching the suffragists parade. The informant was quite right. It seemed to those of us who attempted to march
10 for our idea that day that the whole world was there—packed closely on Pennsylvania Avenue.

The purpose of the procession was to dramatize in numbers the fact that women wanted to vote. What politicians had not been able to get through their minds we would give them through their eyes—often a powerful substitute. Our
15 first task seemed simple: to show that thousands of women wanted immediate action on their long delayed enfranchisement. This we did.

The Administration, without intending it, played into the hands of the women from this moment. The women had been given a permit to march. Inadequate police protection allowed roughs to attack them and all but break up the pageant.
20 The fact of ten thousand women marching with banners and bands for this idea was startling enough to wake up the government and the country, but not so startling as ten thousand women manhandled by irresponsible crowds because of police indifference.

An investigation was demanded and a perfunctory one held. The police
25 administration was exonerated, but when the storm of protest had subsided the Chief of Police was quietly retired to private life.

A few days later the first deputation of suffragists ever to appear before a President in order to enlist his support waited upon President Wilson. Alice Paul led the deputation. The President received the deputation in the White House
30 Offices. When the women entered they found five chairs arranged in a row with one chair in front, like a classroom. All confessed to being frightened when the President came in and took his seat at the head of the class. The President said he had no opinion on the subject of woman suffrage; that he had never given it any thought; and that above all it was his task to see that Congress concentrated
35 on the currency revision and the tariff reform. It is recorded that the President was somewhat taken aback when Miss Paul addressed him during the course of the interview with this query, "But Mr. President, do you not understand that the Administration has no right to legislate for currency, tariff, and any other reform without first getting the consent of women to these reforms?"

40 "Get the consent of women?" It was evident that this course had not heretofore occurred to him.

"This subject will receive my most careful consideration," was President Wilson's first suffrage promise.

He was given time to "consider" and a second deputation went to him, and still
45 a third, asking him to include the suffrage amendment in his message to the new
Congress assembling the following month.

He flatly said there would be no time to consider suffrage for women. But
the "unreasonable" women kept right on insisting that the liberty of half the
American people was paramount to tariff and currency. President Wilson's
50 first session of Congress came together April 7th, 1913. The opening day was
marked by the suffragists' second mass demonstration. This time women
delegates representing every one of the 435 Congressional Districts in the
country bore petitions from the constituencies showing that the people "back
home" wanted the amendment passed. The delegates marched on Congress.
55 The same day the amendment which bears the name of Susan B. Anthony, who
drafted it in 1875, was reintroduced into both houses of Congress.

The month of May saw monster demonstrations throughout the country, with
the direct result that in June the Senate Committee on Suffrage made the first
favorable report made by that committee in twenty-one years, thereby placing it
60 on the Senate calendar for action.

Not relaxing the pressure for a day we organized the third great demonstration
on the last of July when a petition signed by hundreds of thousands of citizens
was brought to the Senate asking that body to pass the national suffrage
amendment. Women from all parts of the country mobilized in the countryside of
65 Maryland. The delegation motored in gaily decorated automobiles to Washington
and went to the Senate, where the entire day was given over to suffrage
discussion.

Twenty-two senators spoke in favor of the amendment. Three spoke against it.
For the first time in twenty-six years suffrage was actually debated in
70 Congress. That day was historic.

1. One of the main purposes of the passage is to:

   A. expose Woodrow Wilson's opposition to women's suffrage.
   B. describe how the amendment for women's suffrage was passed in Congress.
   C. demonstrate the unjust treatment of suffragists by the government.
   D. show how the persistence of the suffragists brought the suffrage debate to government.

2. The author's point of view is that of:

   F. a feminist historian.

   G. an opponent of women's suffrage.

   H. a participant in the events described.

   J. a leader of the deputation that met with the president.

3. The implication of the police chief's retirement in lines 24–26 is that:

   A. he manhandled some of the parading suffragists.

   B. he was ultimately responsible for the lack of protection at the parade.

   C. the government publicly laid the blame on his shoulders.

   D. he opposed the exoneration of the police force.

4. The author most likely uses the comparison of the suffragists' meeting with the president to a classroom in order to suggest that:

   F. the president planned to teach the suffragists.

   G. the president sought to intimidate the suffragists through a show of force.

   H. the White House staff thought the suffragists were schoolchildren.

   J. the president and his staff treated the suffragists in a condescending manner.

5. According to the passage, President Wilson's initial response to the deputation of suffragists was one of:

   A. sympathetic concern.

   B. intellectual consideration.

   C. naive bewilderment.

   D. disinterested disdain.

The directions explain your job: to choose the correct answer to all the questions in the time allotted (35 minutes). Although you'll see four types of passages on test day, the strategies and step method you'll use will always be the same (more on those things later in this Intensive). The directions also tell you that you can jump around within the test. Let's take a look at the passage types in more detail.

Passage Types

Each of the four passages is approximately 750 words long. There are four types, and they always appear in this order:

- Prose Fiction
- Social Science
- Humanities
- Natural Science

The ten questions that follow each passage are never based on outside knowledge; all the information you need to answer them is in the passages.

PROSE FICTION

The Prose Fiction passage is usually an excerpt from a novel or short story. You should approach this passage as you would an assignment for your high school English class, not as you would a book you read in your spare time. What we mean is: When you read fiction for pleasure, you may be tempted to read simply for the story. Yet while the plot is an important element of most fiction, and one on which the questions will test you, it is certainly not the only element. We'll talk more about this passage type in the Special Advice for Prose Fiction section.

SOCIAL SCIENCE

The Social Science passage can cover a variety of subjects, ranging from anthropology to economics to politics. All of the subjects that appear in the Social Science passage essentially deal with the ways societies and civilization work, and most of them have a political context and an analytical tone.

HUMANITIES

The Humanities passage covers cultural matters, particularly art and literature. Like Social Science, this passage tends to be written analytically or journalistically.

NATURAL SCIENCE

The Natural Science passage presents scientific arguments or experiments and explains the reasoning behind them and their significance. The passage is usually heavy on facts and scientific theories.

ESSENTIAL CONCEPTS

Everyday reading is different from ACT reading, mostly because your everyday reading doesn't conclude with a set of multiple-choice questions asking you to remember details, draw inferences, or figure out the author's main idea. The key to ACT reading is to identify the following features of every passage you encounter:

1. Topic and Scope
2. Purpose and Main Idea
3. Tone

Essential Concept #1: Topic and Scope

The *topic* is the subject matter treated in a passage. The *scope* is the breadth of the topic covered in the passage. In our sample passage, the topic is the history of the women's suffrage movement. The questions will test whether you picked up on the *specific aspect* of the women's suffrage movement that the passage covers. On your own, go back to the X-ray and see if you can come up with a definition of the Wilson passage's scope. Then look at our chart to see how your answer matches up.

EXAMPLE OF TOPIC'S SCOPE	DESCRIPTION OF SCOPE
Civil rights	way, way too broad
Women's suffrage	way too broad
The history of the women's suffrage movement	too broad
The history of the women's suffrage movement under the Wilson administration	just right
Wilson's role in the women's suffrage movement	too narrow
The nature of the first meeting between suffragists and Wilson	way too narrow
The passage of the constitutional amendment granting the vote to women	off topic (the passage stops long before that)
Popular objections to the women's suffrage movement	off topic

One way to think of scope is to compare it to the frame of a photograph. If you want to photograph your house, you'll certainly want something in between a satellite photo of the entire Earth (too broad) and an electron micrograph of the wood on your front door (too narrow). And you don't want a picture of someone else's house or of, say, the White House or the Empire State Building ("off topic"). You'll want just the front of the house with a little space on all sides to show a bit of the yard and trees.

Lots of ACT questions require you to know what the passage covers and what it doesn't. Other questions require you to identify the author's focus or concerns, and anything outside the scope of the passage can't be a focus or concern of the author.

The correct answer will always be in line with the topic and scope of the passage: Distractors (answer choices designed to distract your attention from the right answer) that are "out in left field"—i.e., outside the scope—are almost always wrong.

Essential Concept #2: Purpose and Main Idea

The *purpose* of the passage is the reason the author is writing. Every passage has a purpose, and some authors write to express a specific *main idea*. The main idea of a passage is the central point that the author is making. It is a clear expression of the topic and scope, along with the author's particular take on that topic and scope.

Our sample passage basically chronicles certain important events in the history of women's suffrage, beginning with a march held the day before Wilson's inauguration and ending on the day when women's suffrage was first debated in Congress. The passage primarily shows how persistent demonstrations ultimately brought the suffrage movement to Congress.

Some ACT questions directly ask about the author's purpose and the main idea. In our X-ray's sample questions, question 1 tests your understanding of the passage's purpose (more on how to answer it in the Big Five Question Types section). Even for those questions that are not explicitly "global," knowing the main idea/purpose can help you eliminate wrong choices. For example, if you're asked for a statement with which the author will agree, the correct answer will be consistent with the purpose of the passage. Wrong answers often conflict with the author's purpose or the main idea.

Essential Concept #3: Tone

Tone is based both on a passage's style and on the particular words used in the passage. The way an author uses language indicates the author's attitude toward his or her subject matter. Tone may be subjective, objective, positive, negative, neutral, or one of a whole range of adjectives.

In the Wilson passage, the author is definitely opinionated and has a clear sense that Wilson's lack of knowledge and interest in the women's suffrage movement represented a moral failing on Wilson's part.

Like purpose and main idea, tone is often tested directly. Knowing the author's tone helps you answer other questions, such as questions about the author's point of view (question 2 in our sample). Remember too that correct answers to *all* questions tend to agree with the author's tone. Incorrect answers conflict with the author's tone.

ESSENTIAL STRATEGIES

Now that we've covered what you should be looking for as your read the ACT passages, it's time to explain how to use a few techniques to improve your performance. In this section, we go over the strategies to use on the Reading Test.

The crux of your ACT Reading strategy is your ability to read well—that is, with speed and without sacrificing comprehension. Here's what to do on the test:

- Remember the Passage Order
- Read the Passage Before the Questions
- Skim
- Identify Essential Concepts

- Outline
- Make a Prediction
- Eliminate Extreme Answers
- Use the Reading Test Step Method

Remember the Passage Order

As we explained, the Reading Test will always give you a Prose Fiction passage, followed by Social Science, Humanities, and Natural Science passages. Don't feel as if you have to read the four passages in that order. Instead, tackle the passage that's easiest for you, saving the hardest passage for last.

If possible, decide ahead of time how many passages you want to tackle. (Use your performance on the Practice Set at the end of this Intensive to help you decide which passages to attempt on test day.) You can get a better score by doing well on three passages and guessing on the fourth than you would by reading all four and struggling. Don't be afraid to skip a passage if you won't have time to do it justice.

Read the Passage Before the Questions

Read the passage first and save the questions until you're done reading. Some test-prep books tell you to read the questions first, but we disagree. Imagine trying to remember what ten questions ask while reading an unfamiliar passage, simultaneously trying to get the gist of the content and look for answers.

"Passage first, questions after" is really just common sense. Think of the passage as a room and the answers to the questions as objects within the room. If you follow our strategy and tackle the passage first, you'll have turned on the lights and gotten a sense of the room's layout, making the objects much easier to find.

Skim

Read the passage quickly and lightly for a general understanding. Pay active attention to what's going on, but don't get bogged down trying to memorize every detail. Rather than focusing on every single word, focus your attention on getting the gist of what's happening, then go to the questions.

The author uses specific facts to support an argument, but as you read, you should be more concerned with their cumulative effect (i.e., the larger argument) than with the specific facts themselves. If you get to a point in a passage where the author lists a bunch of facts to support an idea, you can make a quick note of the list in the margin for future reference (for more on this, be sure to read the section on outlining).

The only time you should slow down and go back is if you lose the flow of the passage—if you realize you don't know what's happening, what's being argued, or what in the world that entire last paragraph was about.

Identify Essential Concepts

As you read, think about the passage's topic and scope, purpose and main idea, and tone. You might even jot these down in the margins of your test booklet so that they stay utmost in your mind.

Here are our notes on the Essential Concepts of the Wilson passage:

Topic & Scope	The history of the women's suffrage movement under the Wilson administration
Purpose	Explain events that led to debate of suffrage movement in Congress
Main Idea	Persistent demonstrations ultimately brought the suffrage movement to Congress
Tone	Impassioned, opinionated

After you finish the passage, go to the questions. Your notes about the "big picture" will help you answer the general questions dealing with main points, point of view, and tone.

Outline

In addition to your notes about the Essential Concepts, you should also mark up the passage, underlining key phrases and making notes about each paragraph. Later you can use your underlines and notes as a map through the passage, so that you don't waste time covering passage territory for a second time.

Underline the topic sentence of each paragraph; doing so will help you keep on top of the argument's direction. Write "ex" or "x" where the author gives examples that support his or her argument. You might also use check marks or asterisks to note key phrases or ideas. Do whatever works for you as long as your scribbles, doodles, and underlines form an outline that lets you quickly identify the passage's important points. Don't try to provide a complete reference guide to the passage. Your outline is meant to prevent you from getting distracted and to give you a quick summary of the passage's key points.

Here's our version of the margin notes/outline:

Intro	Book pub. in 1920
Paragraph 1	Wilson's inauguration = no people
Paragraph 2	Everyone watching suffragist parade
Paragraph 3	Up to W to decide about women/vote
Paragraph 4	Author involved in action (circle the word us)
Paragraph 5	Women marching, b/c want right to vote
Paragraph 6	No police, so protesters get roughed up; public mad
Paragraph 7	Chief retires — bad scene
Paragraph 8	Group goes to W, "classroom"
Paragraph 9	W shocked
Paragraph 10	W to think about it
Paragraph 11	More groups visit W, want amendment

Paragraph 12	Another demonstration, W not very jazzed about woman vote
Paragraph 13	Demonstrations everywhere, Congress — good rep.
Paragraph 14	Senate, big demons.
Paragraph 15	Suffrage debate — first time

Notice how the outline uses incomplete sentences and abbreviations (*W*, *demons*.). As long as your outline provides you with a clear road map to the passage, anything goes. Don't worry about grammar or spelling.

Make a Prediction

This strategy applies to many ACT questions. Making a prediction about the answer as you read the question reduces the likelihood that you'll fall for traps. But it's particularly helpful on the Reading Test because the questions are often long and wordy, which can make this section quite challenging. If you can formulate your own answer, you'll stay focused and not get caught up in answer choices that are there to distract you.

So before going back to the passage, articulate to yourself exactly what the question is asking. Don't look at the answers. Instead, try to formulate an answer in your own words. Then quickly scan the answer choices and choose the one that best matches your version.

Eliminate Extreme Answers

We want to say a few things about the answer choices you'll see before we talk about the step method you should use. In fact, we want to point out a key feature of the answer choices: Choices with "extreme" language are usually wrong, regardless of the question type.

Look at the following chart:

TIME	SPACE OR AMOUNT
Never	None
Rarely	A little/few
Sometimes	Some
Often/frequently	A lot/most
Always	All

The extreme terms are at the top and bottom of this chart; the middle terms are more measured and therefore more likely to be correct when applied to any statement.

Another term to watch out for is *only*. This doesn't quite fit into the chart above, but it nevertheless has a very restrictive meaning—and it's "extreme" in the sense we're discussing now. For example, the statement "The Beatles were the only worthwhile rock group that was active in the 1960s" is pretty extreme. All you would need to do to refute that statement is present a halfway-decent argument that any other 1960s rock group was "worthwhile." Beware of the word *only*.

Use the Reading Test Step Method

Use the following step method every time you attempt an ACT passage and its questions. As you'll see, it incorporates some of the Essential Strategies we just discussed.

Step 1: Skim and Outline the Passage First.

Step 2: Answer Specific Questions.

Step 3: Answer General Questions.

Before we show you how the steps work, we want to remind you of the importance of staying focused. You need to focus on the ACT passages as you would on something you really cared about. Do whatever you can to engage with the passage, and try to channel your manufactured passion into better focus and attention to detail. Taking notes, outlining, and identifying the Essential Concepts will help you stay in the moment; they'll also help you perform the various steps.

Now let's see how the steps work.

Step 1: Skim and Outline the Passage First. Concentrate on the introduction, the conclusion, the first main paragraph, and the first and last sentences of every subsequent paragraph. Don't forget to take notes! Again, your notes should be similar to the ones we took on the Wilson passage earlier in this Intensive.

Step 2: Answer Specific Questions. Specific questions refer directly to words or lines in the passage. Before rushing back to the passage, articulate to yourself exactly what the question is asking. When you're clear on the question, go to the specific area in the passage and read just the few lines above and below it to get a sense of the context. Come up with your own answer to the question, then find the answer choice that matches yours. We explain more about specific questions in the section on the Big Five Question Types later in this Intensive.

Step 3: Answer General Questions. General questions ask about broad aspects of the passage, such as its main idea, tone, and argument. You should be able to answer them without looking back at the passage; instead, use your notes and outline to answer general questions. We explain more about general questions in our discussion of question types in the next section.

As you tackle Steps 2 and 3, remember that every question is worth the same amount. So don't spend too much time on any one question. Decide which questions are worth tackling. Some questions are quick kills, and some take forever. Some are easy and some are hard. Scoop up the easy points quickly and only then try the tough stuff. Eliminating a few choices and guessing quickly, rather than leaving questions blank, will generally help your score.

THE BIG FIVE QUESTION TYPES

The Reading Test evaluates a set of skills you've acquired rather than subjects you've learned, namely your ability to read and process written information. Keep this in mind as we cover the Big Five Question Types you'll see on ACT Reading:

QUESTION TYPE	YOUR TASK
1. Specific Detail	Find something specific within the passage.
2. Point of View	Identify how the writer views his or her subject.
3. Big Picture/Purpose	Identify the passage's purpose or main idea.
4. Comparison and Analogy	Compare or make an analogy between two things.
5. Inference	Take something given in the passage and use it to figure out something else.

We've ordered these question types from most specific to most general.

1. Specific Detail

> **5.** According to the passage, President Wilson's initial response to the deputation of suffragists was one of:
>
> **A.** sympathetic concern.
> **B.** intellectual consideration.
> **C.** naive bewilderment.
> **D.** disinterested disdain.

These are perhaps the most straightforward and most common questions you'll encounter. As the name suggests, these questions ask you to find specific details within the passage. Answer Specific Detail questions *before* you answer general questions (like Big Picture). When you get to a question on a specific detail, don't immediately look at the answer choices to avoid being influenced by "trick" answers.

If you're directed to the passage, go back and read the referenced lines. Although this question doesn't refer to specific lines, we're nevertheless referred back to the passage: We need to find the place where the author discusses Wilson's *initial response* to the suffragists. Though we're not directed back to the passage per se, we should still quickly skim the passage to find where the author discusses Wilson's response to the suffragists, or lines 35–49. In fact, the first line of paragraph 8 specifically mentions *the first deputation of suffragists*. Bingo.

As always, try to generate a potential answer *without* looking at the answer choices. Scanning the paragraph quickly, we come to the following line: *The president said he had no opinion on the subject*. Basically, the president felt nothing. Later in the paragraph, the author tells us that Wilson was *somewhat taken aback*. That's pretty negative, so a good prediction might be something like "not interested."

Once we have a prediction in place, we can check out the answer choices, and select the one that matches our prediction. In this case, **D**. Wilson is definitely not portrayed as sympathetic or concerned in the passage, so **A** can go. Make sure not to mistake the tone of the section. When the author describes how Wilson promised to consider the issue, she puts "consider" in quotation marks to indicate that it's a false word: He never intended to consider the issue, but he wanted to get the women off his back. That gets rid of **B**. When he asks the question, *Get the consent of women?* he is not showing naive bewilderment, **C**; he's indicating how preposterous the suggestion seems to him. Wilson's reaction as he traveled to his inauguration was closer to naive bewilderment, but that's a different part of the passage.

Here's another example of a Specific Detail question:

6. According to the passage, violence directed against the parading suffragists resulted from:

    F. a lack of proper policing of the event.
    G. the crowd's resentment of the suffragists.
    H. the police's effort to agitate the crowd.
    J. the suffragists' use of inflammatory language.

Use your outline to direct you to the part of the passage that discusses the *parading suffragists*. (Remember to always jot down the main idea of each paragraph as you skim. These jottings will form the basis of your outline.) The answer to this question can be found at the end of the sixth paragraph, where the author writes that women were *manhandled* by the crowd *because of police indifference*. In other words, the police failed to protect the women from the crowd.

With a prediction in place, we can turn to the answer choices. **F** matches our prediction perfectly. As for **G**, there was definitely hostility at play and maybe even resentment, but the author lays the blame on the police, although she never says that the police encouraged the violence, as **H** suggests. As for **J**, we never learn what kind of language they were using or whether it provoked violence.

And here's one last Specific Detail example:

> **7.** The author states that the May demonstrations directly led to:
>
> **A.** the reintroduction of the Susan B. Anthony amendment in Congress.
> **B.** a favorable report made by the Senate Committee on Suffrage.
> **C.** a day of discussion about suffrage in the Senate.
> **D.** twenty-two senators speaking in support of suffrage.

This Specific Detail question tests whether you understand the specific relationship between the *May demonstrations* and the correct answer. Your outline should guide you back to the particular place in the passage that discusses the May demonstrations. Line 57 talks about the *monster demonstrations* that led to a *favorable report* on suffrage. The lines in the paragraph give the answer, so now it's just a question of finding the best match among the answer choices.

While all of the answer choices give events that occurred after periods of protesting, only the May demonstrations, according to the passage, resulted in the writing of a favorable report by the Senate Committee on Suffrage. **B** is correct.

2. Point of View

> **2.** The author's point of view is that of:
>
> **F.** a feminist historian.
> **G.** an opponent of women's suffrage.
> **H.** a participant in the events described.
> **J.** a leader of the deputation that met with the president.

Point of View (POV) questions on the three nonfiction passages will ask you to identify how the writer views his or her subject. POV questions on the fiction passage will ask you to identify the point of view of the narrator, who is a made-up person used by the writer to tell the story. This question type doesn't come up much following the Prose Fiction passage, but it is fairly common following nonfiction passages.

As you read the passage, consider whether the writer's argument seems to support or attack the passage's subject, and pay attention to the language used. The writer's tone will be a good indication of his or her feelings about the subject. Be sure to note the writer's tone in your outline.

This question type can be general, as in the above example, or more specific. If the POV question asks about the overall tone or point of view, save it for Step 3. If it asks about the tone or POV in a certain part of the passage, answer it right away, in Step 2. No matter what, always remember to form a prediction before checking out the answer choices.

In general, the author seems to support the cause and people depicted in the passage. Let's look at the answer choices: Cut **G** because we know the author supports the cause. Cut **F**, too, because there is little implication that the author is a historian. It is clear from the passage that the author lived during the events she described and, in fact, participated in them. She uses *we* several times. Both **H** and **J** place the author in the events described, but now things get tricky: You must figure out the extent of her involvement. She never suggests that she led the deputation that met with the president. The point of view of that paragraph is of one who had the events described to her, so the correct answer to this question is **H**: The author participated in the events, but she did not participate in the deputation.

Let's look at another POV question:

> **8.** The author's tone when discussing the "'unreasonable' women" in lines 48–49 can best be described as:
>
> **F.** sarcastic.
> **G.** contemptuous.
> **H.** objective.
> **J.** insincere.

As always, when given specific line numbers, go back to the passage and re-read a little before and a little after the given lines. Doing so reminds us that the author has placed the word *unreasonable* in quotation marks to indicate that it is a quotation, an adjective that people other than she would use to describe these women. Because she does incorporate it into her writing without comment (other than the quotation marks), its use can best be described as *sarcastic*.

Essentially, the author writes *unreasonable* while meaning something else; in fact, she most likely considers these women to be anything but unreasonable. The best answer to this question is **F** because it comes the closest to capturing the author's intention of saying one thing while meaning another. **J** suggests a different motive in writing *unreasonable*: deceit. The use of *unreasonable* in the passage is supposed to draw even greater attention to the author's belief that the women were quite reasonable; there is no deceit intended.

3. Big Picture/Purpose

1. One of the main purposes of the passage is to:

   A. expose Woodrow Wilson's opposition to women's suffrage.
   B. describe how the amendment for women's suffrage was passed in Congress.
   C. demonstrate the unjust treatment of suffragists by the government.
   D. show how the persistence of the suffragists brought the suffrage debate to government.

These questions ask about the passage as a whole, usually focusing on why the author wrote it or what the overarching main idea is—that's why we call them "Big Picture/Purpose." Correct answers will capture the scope and tone of the passage. Wrong answers will focus too heavily on details or distort the author's purpose. Big Picture/Purpose questions are general questions, so you should save them for the end, Step 3.

Here's where your notes and the Essential Concepts come in especially handy: The passage describes some events beginning with a march held the day before Wilson's inauguration and ending on the day when women's suffrage was first debated in Congress. As we discussed earlier, the passage primarily shows how persistent demonstrations ultimately brought the suffrage movement to Congress. And there's our potential answer.

Although the author doesn't seem overly fond of Wilson, her main purpose is not to "expose" him in any way, so **A** can go. The passage never deals with the actual granting of suffrage, so eliminate **B**. Similarly, although the author doesn't seem to condone the treatment of suffragists, she doesn't seek to prove any arguments about the unjustness of their treatment, so **C** can go too. That leaves **D**, the correct answer: The passage primarily shows how persistent demonstrations ultimately brought the suffrage movement to Congress.

4. Comparison and Analogy

4. The author most likely uses the comparison of the suffragists' meeting with the president to a classroom in order to suggest that:

   F. the president planned to teach the suffragists.
   G. the president sought to intimidate the suffragists through a show of force.
   H. the White House staff thought the suffragists were schoolchildren.
   J. the president and his staff treated the suffragists in a condescending manner.

This question type asks you to make comparisons, usually between different viewpoints or data, or to draw an analogy between two seemingly dissimilar things. Sometimes Comparison and Analogy questions will hinge on your understanding of metaphor, whereby an author won't explicitly say that something *is like* something else but will instead *imply* that one thing is like another thing. You'll almost certainly see this question type after the Social Science and Natural Science passages. Because these questions require an understanding of the passage as a whole, we recommend you save them for Step 3.

Begin by going back to the passage to find the description of the meeting—beginning around line 30. As the author describes the situation, the suffragists entered to find the chairs set up *like a classroom* with President Wilson seated *at the head of the class*. The suffragists were there to talk to the president about issues of great importance, so your answer should reflect the tense, uncomfortable atmosphere (later in the paragraph, we learn that the president was *taken aback*).

F and **H** are incorrect; there is no suggestion of teaching or schoolchildren in the passage—the classroom is used only as a means of comparison. **G** seems possible, although the arrangement of the furniture is not exactly a show of force. The better answer to this question is **J** because it demonstrates the point of the furniture arrangement: to demean the suffragists.

5. Inference

3. The implication of the police chief's retirement in lines 24–26 is that:

    A. he manhandled some of the parading suffragists.

    B. he was ultimately responsible for the lack of protection at the parade.

    C. the government publicly laid the blame on his shoulders.

    D. he opposed the exoneration of the police force.

Inference questions ask for *implied information*. They want you to take a piece of information given in the passage and use it to figure out something else. Because the answers are not given explicitly within the passage, these questions are often significantly more difficult than Specific Detail questions. But they're just as common, so you need to get a handle on them. These tend to be general questions in the sense that Inference questions require you to understand the *entire* passage, even if the question refers to a specific part of that passage, as in our example. As a general rule, save them for Step 3.

An *inference* is best understood as an unobserved fact that one believes must be true given other observed facts. For example:

FACTS	INFERENCE
When I went to sleep last night, there was no snow on the ground.	It snowed while I was asleep.
When I woke up this morning, there was snow on the ground.	

Some inferences are not as logically necessary as the snow example. They are merely statistically possible or logically probable. Take a look at these examples:

> **Fact:** Most of the school's students had complained that the dress code was too strict.

Fact: The new principal changed the dress code to make it less strict.

Inference: Student complaints led to the change in the dress code.

Well, that might be the case. The reasoning used to infer that student complaints led to the policy change makes sense. But there are other possible reasons, each of which is based on a hidden assumption:

Hidden Assumption 1: The school's administration takes student complaints into account.
Other Potential Reason: Parents complained on behalf of their children. The school's administration took these complaints more seriously.

Hidden Assumption 2: The new principal changed the policy in response to student complaints rather than out of his own preexisting beliefs.
Other Potential Reason: The new principal believes that what students wear doesn't have much of an impact on how they learn.

Hidden Assumption 3: The new code reflects student concerns.
Other Potential Reason: Maybe the dress code is technically less strict but not in the ways that mattered to the students.

Many questions will ask you to make an inference based on the information given in the passage. You'll need to decide which inferences are valid and which are not. Proper inferences tend to be closer to the snow example than to the dress code example—that is, more logically necessary than statistically probable.

Inference questions frequently use verbs such as *suggest, infer, imply,* and *indicate.* Take a look at question 3 again. Here, we don't have a verb, but we do have the noun form of the verb *imply*: *implication.* The test makers tell us to review particular lines, 24–26. That makes life easier. Remember to always read a few lines above and below the specific lines. The paragraph in question discusses what happened to the police and the chief after the protest.

The author states that although the police force was exonerated of guilt in the manhandling of the suffragists, the police chief quietly left office after the investigation. His retirement suggests his culpability in this case—regardless of whether it was directly his fault. So a good prediction is that he felt guilty or responsible.

Time to compare our prediction to the choices: **A** is too specific. We don't know that he did anything himself. **B** is correct, but let's check out **C** and **D** just to make sure: **C** is contradicted by the passage. The chief retired quietly. **D** is outside the scope of the passage. We don't know what he did.

When asked for an inference, most test takers will pick something that might be possible, and perhaps even suggested, but that doesn't technically qualify as an inference. Always look for the strongest support from the text for any inference you make. An inference that can't be supported by the passage can't be the correct answer.

Here's another Inference question:

> 9. In the sixth paragraph (lines 17–23) the author implies that the administration "played into the hands of the women" by:
>
> A. giving the women a permit to march.
> B. demanding an investigation after the parade.
> C. unintentionally generating publicity for the suffragists.
> D. considering the suffragists' demands.

Begin by taking a look at the lines referred to by the question. In the first sentence of that paragraph, the author states that the administration played into the women's hands *without intending it*. That phrase lets you know that the administration's actions accidentally benefited the suffragists, so our answer should reflect that.

Let's look at the choices: You can also use the phrase *without intending it* so eliminate **A** and **B**. Both of those represent actions *intentionally* performed by the government in fairness to the suffragists. **C** works as a probable answer to this question because it uses the word *unintentionally*. **D** is never implied in the passage. **C** is correct.

And here's one more example of an Inference question:

> **10.** One can reasonably infer that the author believes tariff reform and currency revision are:
>
> **F.** as important as suffrage for women.
> **G.** obstructions to the liberty of half the American people.
> **H.** empty and unfair without women's votes on the issues.
> **J.** equally important issues to men and women.

To tackle this question, we need to first find where the author mentions *tariff reform and currency revision*: Paragraph 8. In general, the author's views seem to be in line with the views she attributes to the suffrage leaders in the passage. The author describes how Alice Paul tells a surprised Wilson that the government has no right to legislate for any reform without women's consent to the reforms. It is safe to assume that the author feels the same way as Paul, whom she portrays favorably in the passage. Scanning the choices, we can see that **H** best captures this.

SPECIAL ADVICE FOR PROSE FICTION

3

Before we get to the practice questions, let's talk briefly about the fiction passage. The only major difference between fiction and nonfiction passages is that fiction passages are not structured as rigidly as nonfiction passages are. When reading the ACT Prose Fiction passage, keep the following question in mind: "Who is doing what to whom and how does it make everyone, including the narrator, feel?" Here's a recap of fiction's main elements, any or all of which might show up in the questions that follow the fiction passage:

- **The narrator.** The "voice" that's telling the story.
- **The characters.** Keep in mind who's who, and what their relationships are (mother/daughter, friends, husband/wife, etc.).
- **The plot.** Not much can actually transpire in a passage of roughly 750 words. Events will be apparent. The most you'll be asked to do is read between the lines of what characters say to one another, which is a skill you already use every day. ("Jane said I look good today. Does she really mean this, or was it a sarcastic dig?")
- **The way the author uses language to convey states of mind and events.** Looking for this is like identifying the author's purpose in nonfiction passages.

As you read, circle names of characters, key dialogue, crucial images—do whatever it takes to stay physically and mentally engaged. At the very least, aim to get an idea of what happens where in the passage so that when you hit the questions you'll have some idea of where you might need to go in the passage to puzzle out a particular item.

PRACTICE SET

This practice set has one Humanities passage and one Natural Science passage, each with question. Don't forget to employ the step method as you tackle the questions.

PASSAGE I

HUMANITIES: This passage is adapted from Henry James's "*The Art of Fiction.*"

The only reason for the existence of a novel is that it does compete with life. When it ceases to compete as the canvas of the painter competes, it will have arrived at a very strange pass. It is not expected of the picture that it will make itself humble in order to be forgiven; and the analogy between the art of

5 the painter and the art of the novelist is complete. Their inspiration is the same, their process (allowing for the different quality of the vehicle) is the same, their success is the same. They may learn from each other, they may explain and sustain each other. Their cause is the same, and the honor of one is the honor of another.

10 As the picture is reality, so the novel is history. That is the only general description (which does it justice) that we may give the novel. But history also is allowed to compete with life; it is not, any more than painting, expected to apologize. The subject-matter of fiction is stored up likewise in documents and records, and if it will not give itself away, it must speak with assurance, with the

15 tone of the historian.

Certain accomplished novelists have a habit of giving themselves away, which must often bring tears to the eyes of people who take their fiction seriously. I was lately struck, in reading over many pages of Anthony Trollope, with his want of discretion in this particular. In a digression, he concedes to the

20 reader that he and his trusting friend are only "making believe." He admits that the events he narrates have not really happened, and that he can give his narrative any turn the reader may like best.

Such a betrayal of a sacred office seems to me a terrible crime; it is what I mean by the attitude of apology. It implies that the novelist is less occupied in

25 looking for the truth than the historian. To represent and illustrate the past, the actions of men, is the task of either writer. The only difference that I can see is, in proportion as he succeeds, to the honor of the novelist, consisting as it does in his having more difficulty in collecting his evidence, which is so far from being purely literary. It seems to me to give him a great character.

30   It is of all this evidently that Mr. Besant is full when he insists upon the fact
that fiction is one of the fine arts, deserving in its turn of all the honors and
emoluments that have hitherto been reserved for the successful professions of
music, poetry, painting, architecture. It is excellent that he should have struck this
note, for his doing so indicates that his proposition may be to many people
35   a novelty. I suspect that in addition to the people to whom it has never occurred
that a novel ought to be artistic, there are a great many others who, if this
principle were urged upon them, would be filled with an indefinable mistrust.
        "Art" is supposed, in certain circles, to have some vaguely injurious effect
upon those who make it an important consideration. It is assumed to be opposed
40   to morality, to amusement, to instruction. Literature should be either instructive
or amusing, and there is in many minds an impression that these artistic
preoccupations contribute to neither end, interfere indeed with both.
        That, I think, represents the manner in which the latent thought of many
people who read novels as an exercise in skipping would explain itself if it
45   were to become articulate. They would argue that a novel ought to be "good,"
but they would interpret this term in a fashion of their own, which would vary
considerably from one critic to another. One would say that being good means
representing virtuous and aspiring characters, placed in prominent positions;
another would say that it depends for a "happy ending" on a distribution at the
50   last of prizes, pensions, husbands, wives, babies, millions, appended paragraphs
and cheerful remarks.
        Another still would say that it means being full of incident and movement, so
that we shall wish to jump ahead, to see who was the mysterious stranger, and if
the stolen will was ever found, and shall not be
55   distracted from this pleasure by any tiresome analysis or "description." But
they would all agree that the "artistic" idea would spoil some of their fun.
        The "ending" of a novel is, for many persons, like that of a good dinner,
a course of dessert and ices, and the artist in fiction is regarded as a sort of
meddlesome doctor who forbids agreeable aftertastes. It matters little that, as a
60   work of art, the novel should really be as little or as much concerned to supply
happy endings as if it were a work of mechanics; the association of ideas,
however incongruous, might easily be too much for it if an eloquent voice were
not sometimes raised to call attention to the fact that it is at once as free and as
serious a branch of literature as any other.

1. In the passage, the author compares the novel to:

    A. painting.
    B. history and painting.
    C. music, poetry, painting, and architecture.
    D. making believe.

2. The author states that the worth of the novel is that it:

    F. competes with life.
    G. competes with painting to capture life.
    H. gives an accurate historical perspective.
    J. belongs to the fine arts.

3. The attitude of apology, mentioned in line 24 most likely refers to:

    A. the novelist's apparent lack of concern for historical truth.
    B. the writings of Anthony Trollope.
    C. the novelist's attempt to please the reader.
    D. the admission in a novel that the described events are made-up.

4. One can reasonably infer from the passage that the novelist takes his evidence from:

    F. his imagination.
    G. documents and records only.
    H. history and the actions of men.
    J. the reader's preference.

5. According to the passage, Mr. Besant believes that:

    A. literature should be recognized as a fine art.
    B. there are many people who do not consider the novel an artistic form.
    C. his ideas are new to many people.
    D. many people mistrust art.

6. The view of art described in lines 38–42 can best be described as:

    F. admiring.
    G. indifferent.
    H. academic.
    J. wary.

7. The main purpose of the next-to-last paragraph (lines 52–56) is to:

    A. present a view of literature as mere amusement.

    B. defend the artistic merit of literature.

    C. illustrate the thinking of people who skip through novels.

    D. describe different ways of reading novels.

8. The author's tone in lines 43–51 suggests that he:

    F. disagrees with the views described in these paragraphs.

    G. agrees with the views described in these paragraphs.

    H. is indifferent to the views detailed in these paragraphs.

    J. finds the views described in these paragraphs convincing without entirely agreeing with them.

9. In the passage the author makes all of the following analogies EXCEPT comparing:

    A. happy endings of novels to dessert.

    B. the literary artist to a meddlesome doctor.

    C. art to mechanics.

    D. the novelist to the painter.

10. Which of the following best states the main point of the passage?

    F. The novel must finally be recognized by both novelists and readers as a form of artistic expression.

    G. When crafting their novels, novelists should use painters and historians as their models.

    H. A work of art is created in the same manner as a work of mechanics.

    J. People who skip through novels do not regard fiction as artistic expression.

PASSAGE II

NATURAL SCIENCE: This passage is adapted from Stacey Dworkin's "*Signing.*"

Some animal activities have become ritualized over the course of evolution so that they now serve a communicative function. Protective reflexes, for example, such as narrowing the eyes and flattening the ears, prepare an animal in danger to protect sense organs. These movements also may indicate fear or anger to other
5 animals. Intention movements such as these are incomplete behavior patterns that provide information about the activity a particular animal is about to perform. A bird will generally crouch, raise its tail, and pull back its head before it takes

flight. If a bird takes flight without first performing these movements, it acts as an alarm signal, and the whole flock will suddenly take flight.

Ritualized behaviors allow for the evolution of a signal by increasing conspicuousness, stereotypy, and separation from its original function. An example of such increasing exaggeration can be found in bower birds. Males decorate their nest with blue objects. They will steal any blue object, including pieces of paper, plastic, and glass. This behavior began as nest building and has evolved to attract females.

The process of ritualization first involves the receiver noticing the correlation between the signal and the actions of the sender. The sender then ritualizes his signal to receive the optimal ideal response from the receiver and the receiver modifies his response to optimally benefit himself. As an example, a dog who is preparing to bite retracts his lips into the familiar growl snarl. This particular behavior began so that the dog does not bite his own lips as he bites. However at some point in evolutionary history, the receiver noticed that the snarling dog presented a danger to him. The signaling dog now notices the receiver often backs down before the fight even begins, and continues retracting his lips as a way to ward off the receiver. However, this ritualization can have a "dog who cried wolf" result, where the receiver will become so accustomed to the snarling without attack that he will no longer retreat.

Signals of conflict, such as that of predator to prey, involve a signaler who intends to manipulate the receiver. The receiver then interprets the signal as a warning sign and evolves resistance. The result is a co-evolutionary arms race, which can lead to increasingly exaggerated signals.

According to Zahavi's handicap principle, in order to be honest, a signal must be costly to the signaler. Thus only the most fit individuals can afford to brandish an honest signal. For females looking for a mate, such a declaration of fitness will identify a particular male as a quality choice.

For this reason, some signals, such as peacock's tails, become extremely exaggerated: males are trying to declare their fitness, since only the toughest males can survive with such a costly, conspicuous tail. Another example is the black bib of dominant male Harris sparrows. Only dominant males have this black bib. An experiment in which males were given a black bib by means of a magic marker showed that that male was attacked by other sparrows. The male with an artificial black bib could not survive the attack; only the fittest males could have the black bib of dominance and not lose fights by challengers.

There is currently a great deal of debate about the validity of the handicap principle, and there is some evidence that the principle does not always hold true. However, in general, costly signals such as peacock tails can serve no other purpose than as honest indicators of fitness.

Cooperation, on the other hand, involves a mutual interest of the signaler and receiver. In terms of cooperation, the signaler and receiver both want to be

50 able to communicate while remaining as little noticed as possible by potential predators. Such inconspicuous signaling offers a distinct selective advantage. Evolution therefore results in "conspiratorial whispers," where both signaler and receiver evolve to make the signal as inconspicuous as possible while still reaching its receiver without alerting unintended receivers.

11. The main idea of the first paragraph (lines 1–9) is that:

  A. signals develop as animals ritualize their behavior.
  B. animals use their reflexive movements to communicate with other animals.
  C. animals' reflexes and movements can often assume a communicative function.
  D. animals respond physically to danger.

12. The passage states that the first step of ritualization involves the:

  F. sender's ritualization of his signal to receive an optimal response.
  G. recognition by the receiver of a relationship between the sender's actions and the signal.
  H. modification of the receiver's response for optimal benefit.
  J. increased conspicuousness of the sender's activity.

13. The author states that a "dog who cried wolf" situation results when:

  A. a signal becomes so familiar that it fails to affect the receiver.
  B. a signal is used to create an impression of strength and viciousness.
  C. an animal assumes the appearance of a stronger animal.
  D. an animal uses a signal indiscriminately.

14. According to the passage, the male bower bird attracts a female mate by:

  F. building a nest decorated with blue objects.
  G. stealing blue objects.
  H. demonstrating fitness.
  J. raising its tail before flight.

15. In the passage, the author uses all of the following animals as examples EXCEPT:

  A. dogs.
  B. cats.
  C. peacocks.
  D. sparrows.

16. The primary conclusion of the experiment described in lines 39–43 is that:

    F. altering the physical appearance of male Harris sparrows could also alter their fitness.

    G. male Harris sparrows given false black bibs were instantly attacked by sparrows with real black bibs.

    H. male Harris sparrows with black bibs are constantly faced with challenges to their fitness.

    J. the black bib on a male Harris sparrow is a sign of dominance and fitness.

17. The passage suggests that the main difference between signals of conflict and cooperation is that:

    A. signals of conflict are less conspicuous than signals of cooperation.

    B. only signals of conflict involve two-way communication.

    C. signals of cooperation develop from mutual interest and benefit.

    D. signals of cooperation attempt to manipulate receivers.

18. The main purpose of the passage is to:

    F. argue that signals primarily function as indicators of fitness.

    G. explain how signals of conflict operate.

    H. show that animals use a complicated system of signals to attract mates.

    J. describe how communication can occur through animal behavior and appearance.

19. The author would most likely agree that Zahavi's handicap principle:

    A. is fundamentally unsound.

    B. needs to be replaced by a new principle that takes into account derivations from Zahavi's principle.

    C. is questionable but points to a general truth.

    D. accurately explains which signals are honest.

20. According to the passage, all of the following are characteristics of honest signaling except:

    F. it can attract the attention of unwanted receivers, such as predators.

    G. it is constant over time and does not change.

    H. it eventually leads to extremely exaggerated and impractical signals.

    J. after a while, some signals fail to work.

Guided Explanations

1. B

To answer this Specific Detail question, you can immediately eliminate **D** if you remember that the author complains in the third paragraph about the comparison of the novel to making believe. **C** is wrong because the author does not make that comparison; rather, Mr. Besant makes it. In choosing between the remaining answers, remember to pick the best possible answer to the question. While the author certainly does compare the novel to painting throughout the passage, he also compares it to history in paragraph 2.

2. F

The answer to this Specific Detail question is in the first sentence of the passage. There the author states that "the only reason for the existence of a novel is that it does compete with life."

3. D

The *attitude of apology* refers to the desire to make fiction "humble" by making clear the fictional aspect of the novel—to the extent that the novelist diminishes the authority of his writing. Remember to answer Specific Detail questions like this in Step 2.

4. H

The word *infer* tips us off to question type: Inference. The author states that the task of fiction is to represent and illustrate the past, so it is a fair inference that the novelist mines history in researching the novel. **H** is correct because it gives a more general answer than **G**—historical evidence can be found in sources other than documents and records.

5. A

This question asks for *specific information*. While all of the answer choices are mentioned in the fourth paragraph of the passage, the correct answer, **A**, is given in the first sentence of that paragraph. The rest of the answer choices are all suggested by the author of the passage, not by Mr. Besant, later in the paragraph.

6. J

You can answer this Specific Detail question by reading the sentences immediately preceding the lines referred to. There the author states that the notion of an artistic novel would fill certain people with mistrust.

7. C

Your outline should have helped you answer this question quickly. The next-to-last paragraph attempts to articulate the arguments and thoughts of "people who read novels as an exercise in skipping." **A** is incorrect because the author himself does not propose this view, although he does present the thinking behind it. While the author ultimately wants to defend the art of the novel, that defense is not the focus of this paragraph, so **B** is wrong. **D** may sound possible, but it is a vague and unspecific answer. The author discusses a specific approach to reading the novel in this paragraph—the approach that says novels are mere amusement or instruction, insubstantial enough to justify skipping.

8. F

The author does not agree with people who skip through novels. The use of quotation marks to accent certain words heightens the tone of contempt for those kinds of readers. You can also answer this Point of View question just by knowing that the views described in this paragraph are opposed to the arguments the author makes throughout the passage.

9. C

Close reading of the passage will help you answer this question. Obviously, **D** is wrong because the analogy of novelist to painter is dealt with thoroughly in the passage. The remaining answer choices can be found in the last part of the passage. A close reading of the last paragraph will show that **C** is the right answer to this question because it is not an analogy made in the passage—although both art and mechanics are mentioned in the same sentence.

10. F

G and **H** are not points made in the passage, although they incorporate words and phrases used in the passage. **J** is a point made in the passage, but it is primarily made in the second-to-last paragraph. Thus **F** is correct; it sums up the author's argument throughout the passage. Remember to answer Big Picture/Purpose questions like these last.

11. C

This Specific Detail question points you to a specific spot in the passage: The first paragraph deals with the way that physical movements can communicate messages to other animals—whether these messages are intended or not. Although ritualization is mentioned in the first sentence of this paragraph, the paragraph itself does not focus on the link between ritualized behavior and intended signals, so **A** is not the correct answer to this question. Similarly, **B** is incorrect because it suggests that the paragraph deals with intended signals or intended forms of communication. While the paragraph does give examples of how some animals (birds) will respond to moments of danger, that response is not the main focus of the paragraph—it is only an illustrative example—so **D** is also wrong. The correct answer is **C** because it points to the communicative function of physical movement.

12. G

You can find the answer to this Specific Detail question at the beginning of the third paragraph. There the author states that the "process of ritualization first involves the receiver noticing the correlation between the signal and the actions of the sender."

13. A

The story goes that a boy cried wolf so many times that when a wolf finally appeared no one believed his calls. You don't need to know this tale in order to answer this Comparison and Analogy question, but it can help you eliminate **B** and **C** without referring back to the passage. The comparison between the dog and the boy gets a little confusing when you're choosing between **A** and **D**. In the story, the boy cries wolf rather indiscriminately—when there was no real danger. But in the passage, the "dog who cried wolf" situation arises because the dog uses his snarl to warn off attackers so often that attackers learn to ignore the signal.

14. F

The bower bird is discussed in the second paragraph, where the author describes how the male birds will steal blue objects to decorate their nests and how this decoration attracts females. The correct answer to this question is **F** because it is the decoration of the nest, not the stealing of blue objects, that ultimately attracts mates. As always, answer Specific Detail questions like this first.

15. B

The author uses dogs as an example in the third paragraph, and she uses peacocks and sparrows in the sixth paragraph. She never mentions cats. You can note what kinds of evidence or examples an author uses in your outline.

16. J

It is possible to arrive at several conclusions from the black bib experiment, but only one is relevant to the point the author makes in the paragraph. Which of the answer choices seems the most relevant to the author's argument? Make a prediction, then look at the answer. You can eliminate **F** because, according to the experiment, it is incorrect. **G** does not represent a conclusion the author is trying to draw from the experiment; she never touches the idea that sparrows with false bibs are targeted by those with real bibs. **H** is wrong because the experiment (as the author describes it) doesn't deal with the frequency of challenges made against black-bib sparrows. The correct answer to this question is **J** because the author uses the experiment to show that exaggerated signals are usually adopted by only the fittest of a species.

17. C

In the fourth and fifth paragraphs, the author describes how signals of conflict involve the sender's manipulation of unsuspecting receivers, while in the last paragraph she discusses how signals of cooperation involve the mutual cooperation of senders and receivers.

18. J

Hopefully you saved this Big Picture/Purpose question for last. **F** is incorrect because the author begins to discuss the relationship between signals and fitness only toward the end of the passage, and answer **G** is incorrect because signals of conflict are described only in the fourth paragraph. **H** provides a pretty limited answer to this question; the passage often discusses how animals attract mates, but these discussions are usually evidence used to support the main idea of the passage: that animal behavior and appearance serve a communicative purpose.

19. C

The phrase *most likely agree* lets you know that this is an Inference question. In the second-to-last paragraph, the author mentions debate over the handicap principle but says that the principle seems to support general observations about honest signals. Given that, you can rule out **A** and **B**. You should also rule out **D** because the author never implies that the principle is accurate, but she does imply that the principle points to a general truth about animal signals.

20. G

All of the answer choices given are characteristics of honest signaling except **G**. Paragraph 5 explains the evolution of extremely exaggerated signals, and the author devotes considerable space explaining why some signals fail to work. The last paragraph of the passage explains how cooperation can limit the attraction and attention of unwanted receivers, which is a danger and thus characteristic of signaling.

INTENSIVE 4

The Science Test

Science Test X-ray

Essential Strategies

The Big Four Question Types

Special Advice for
Conflicting Viewpoints

Practice Set

THE ACT SCIENCE TEST FEATURES SEVEN PASSAGES AND 40 questions. You have 35 minutes to read the passages and answer the questions that follow. While the Science Test may strike fear in the hearts of even the bravest test takers, much of the intimidation of the test is mere bluff: The test's big words, variables, and fancy graphs disguise simple ideas.

The test makers tell you to expect content covering biology, earth/space sciences, chemistry, and physics on the science passages. In the end, however, the test doesn't measure your *knowledge* of science: It measures your *understanding* of scientific data. Where the data comes from doesn't matter. In other words, *the content is not important.*

This Intensive gives you the tools you need to answer the questions and get the points. We'll begin by looking at a sample passage and a few questions, then we'll discuss the Essential Strategies you'll use and the major types of questions you'll see. We'll conclude, as always, by giving you some practice.

SCIENCE TEST X-RAY

Below is a typical science passage followed by five questions. For now, have a quick look to get comfortable with the format and content.

DIRECTIONS: This test contains seven passages, each accompanied by several questions. You should select the answer choice that best answers each question. Within the total allotted time for the test, you may spend as much time as you wish on each individual passage. Calculator use is not permitted.

If left at rest, a spring will hang at its equilibrium position. If a mass (M) is attached to that spring, the spring will grow in length by a distance known as its displacement (x). A larger mass will create a larger displacement than a small mass.

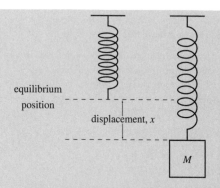

equilibrium position

displacement, x

M

The force (F), in newtons (N), required to return the spring to its equilibrium position is the negative product of the displacement (x) and a spring constant (k), where the negative indicates the direction, not the value, of the force. The spring constant measures the elasticity of a spring: If a spring has a high k, the spring cannot be stretched easily; if a spring has a low k, it can be stretched more easily.

Various masses were attached to two springs with different spring constants, and the force was measured in each of these trials. The energy used (J) returning the spring to its equilibrium position, or Potential Energy (PE), was also measured.

Table 1

Trial	Spring Constant, k	Displacement, x (m)	Force on spring, F (N)	Potential Energy, PE (J)	Mass, M (g)
1	5	1	5	2.5	M_1
2	5	5	25	62.5	M_2
3	5	10	50	250	M_3
4	10	1	10	5	M_4
5	10	5	50	125	M_5
6	10	10	100	500	M_6

1. Which of the following statements about displacement and the force on the spring is consistent with the data in Table 1?

   A. The force on the spring increases as displacement increases.
   B. The force on the spring decreases as displacement increases.
   C. The force on the spring does not change as displacement increases.
   D. The force on the spring increases then decreases as displacement increases.

2. According to the information provided in the introduction and Table 1, which of the following is the largest mass?

   F. M_1
   G. M_3
   H. M_5
   J. M_6

3. If Trial 2 were repeated with a spring with $k = 15$, the displacement of the spring would be:

   A. less than 5.
   B. 5.
   C. between 5 and 15.
   D. greater than 15.

4. Which of the following graphs best represents the change in potential energy with increasing displacement for Trials 1–3?

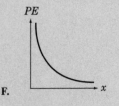

F.

G.

H.

J.

5. What would be the best method of determining how the spring constant affects displacement?

   A. Reproduce Trials 1–6 but use only springs with spring constant $k = 5$.
   B. Reproduce Trials 1–3.
   C. Reproduce Trials 4–6.
   D. Reproduce Trials 1–6 but change the masses in Trials 4–6 to M_1, M_2, and M_3, respectively.

The directions are pretty straightforward: Read the passage, read the questions, select the correct answer. Note too that the directions encourage you to skip around, answering the questions in whatever order works for you. Don't worry about that last sentence regarding calculator use. There is absolutely no need for a calculator on this test, so it doesn't matter that you're not allowed to use one.

Passage Types

On test day, you'll see what the ACT calls "sets": a passage followed by a few questions. There are three types of passages on the test, each of which comes with a different number of questions. You won't need to remember the names of the passages for the ACT, but being able to recognize different passages and knowing what to expect will help you. Here are the types, along with the number of passages and questions per passage:

- **Data Representation: 3 passages, 5 questions per passage.** These passages present you with some data in a paragraph and a chart or table, as in our X-ray. Data Representation questions test your ability to use information presented in the charts.

- **Research Summaries: 3 passages, 6 questions per passage.** These passages present two or three experiments and their results. It might help you to think about Research Summaries as Data Representation placed in the context of a larger experiment.

- **Conflicting Viewpoints: 1 passage, with 7 questions.** This passage presents two or three different theories on an observable phenomenon (such as cloud formation) and requires you to understand the similarities and differences between the viewpoints.

In total, you'll see seven passages and 40 questions. They won't appear in any particular order. As we said earlier, the content of the passages doesn't really matter. As long as you can read the passages and understand the data given by any accompanying graph, chart, and table, you'll be fine. Everything you need to answer the questions is given in the passages.

Note that this Intensive doesn't have our usual list of Essential Concepts. The reason for this goes along with what we said earlier: The Science Test doesn't measure your understanding of science concepts but rather your ability to work with and understand data presented in various forms (in words, charts, tables, graphs, etc.). In other words, the test makers aren't concerned with whether you know that hydrogen molecules bond with an oxygen molecule to form water; instead, they're concerned with whether you can read a description of an experiment and correctly answer questions based on what you've read. Everything you need to answer the questions will be right there in front of you.

In fact, bringing in outside knowledge about science has the potential to confuse you because the questions on the Science Test depend on the data and information given by the passages—not on what you might have learned last week in chemistry class. This Intensive was designed to teach you to understand the passages and answer the questions. So, on that note, read on for our Essential Strategies for the Science Test.

ESSENTIAL STRATEGIES

Read the passage . . . answer the questions that follow. Sound familiar? It should, because it's the same drill as the Reading Test. Like that test, the Science Test gives you a passage, then asks you to answer questions based on that passage. Different content and different questions, of course, but same idea. It follows then that you can use some of the same strategies to conquer the Science Test.

As you work through the Science Test, you'll want to employ the following strategies:

- Don't Be Afraid of the Scientific Jargon
- Scan Quickly for Details
- Take Notes
- Base Your Answers on the Passage
- Use the Science Test Step Method

Don't Be Afraid of the Scientific Jargon

Many people fear the Science Test because of the language used in the passages. But once you get past the language, the questions on this test tend to be fairly straightforward and simple to answer.

The best way to get past the scientific jargon is simply to know that it is jargon. Once you know that the ideas being tested are merely hidden by a thin layer of complicated terms, it becomes much easier to see through that jargon. So when you see scientific terminology that seems confusing, don't panic or get nervous. Take a deep breath and break it down. You'll get through it.

Scan Quickly for Details

When you read the passage for the first time, you should scan quickly for details in order to get a general understanding. That is, you should *skim!* For Data Representation and Research Summaries passages, look at the provided charts to see which factors or variables are represented. At this point, all you want to do is figure out the who and the what. For example, if the passage deals with an experiment, make sure you know what the experiment tests and the goal of the experiment. You shouldn't examine superspecific aspects of the data, such as how the value of one variable changes against another—leave that sort of analysis for when you answer the questions.

Remember that there is very little time on this test, so you shouldn't spend a significant amount of time reading the passages. If you labor excruciatingly over every sentence and piece of data in a passage, you will leave yourself little time to answer the questions. You need to find a balance between reading the passages, looking at any visuals (charts, tables, or graphs), and answering questions.

Take Notes

It's hard to stay focused on science passages, which are filled with data and jargon that can make even the most devoted reader start to drift. Reading quickly for a general overview and taking notes will help keep your mind sharp and on task. Don't try to memorize every piece of data or understand every single variable.

Instead of randomly moving your pencil (or your eyes) across the page, you should answer four key questions about every passage you read:

- What is being tested?
- Why is it being tested?
- What are the variables? That is, what varies or changes?
- What are the factors that stay the same?

Jot down your answers in note form next to the relevant sections of the passage. These notes will form an outline, which you can then refer back to as you tackle the questions. Don't spend too much time making these notes; their main functions are to assist your comprehension of the passage and to jolt your memory when you answer the questions.

Take another look at the "spring" passage from the X-ray. You don't have to know anything about physics to handle this one. You don't have to know what a newton is or why energy used is abbreviated with a *J*. Instead, focus on answering the questions:

- What is being tested?
  Two different spring constants (5 and 10) and some different forces acting on those springs

- Why is it being tested?
  To measure energy used (J) to return spring to equilibrium position; also to measure potential energy

- What are the variables?
  6 diff. masses used, 1 M/trial

- What are the facts that stay the same?
  trials 1–3 = k of 5
  trials 4–6 = k of 10

The strategies of scanning quickly for details and of taking notes have the added advantage of helping you avoid getting bogged down in the sometimes-complicated scientific jargon. We've said it before and we'll say it again: Cutting through the jargon is a major part of doing well on this test.

Use the Science Test Step Method

As we pointed out, there are many similarities between the Reading Test and the Science Test, so we'll borrow Step 1 of the Reading Test Step Method to kick start the Science Test Step Method.

Here's what to do on the Science Test:

Step 1: Skim and Outline the Passage First.

Step 2: Restate the Question.

Step 3: Make a Prediction.

Step 4: Match Your Prediction to the Answer Choices.

Step 1: Skim and Outline the Passage First. By *skim*, we mean "scan quickly for details." And by *outline*, we mean "take notes and answer the key questions" we discussed earlier about aspects of the passages. These activities will help you pay attention; they'll also help you with Step 2.

On test day, read for a general understanding. For Data Representation and Research Summaries passages, begin by skimming the introduction, which will give you a general sense of what the subsequent chart or table might illustrate. Then look at the provided charts to see what factors or variables are represented. You should definitely note the variables in each experiment in the Research Summaries passages.

Don't get hung up on specific aspects of the data, such as how the value of one variable changes against another—leave that sort of analysis for when you answer the questions. Even if a passage completely blows you away, don't take extra time trying to make sense out of it. Hit the questions instead. Even the most brutal passage has a few questions you can answer by simply looking up information.

Step 2: Restate the Question. Once you've completed your first reading of the passage and gotten a sense of what it's about, move on to the questions. Remember that questions generally move from easiest to hardest within a science set, so try to tackle the first few questions first.

Restating the question in your own words lets you cut through the potentially confusing verbiage and get to the heart of what the test makers want you to do. We'll show you more about how to do this when we work through the question types in the next section.

Step 3: Make a Prediction. You'll want to predict the answer to a question before looking at the answer choices. Formulating an answer in your own words helps you avoid the test makers' traps. Science traps tend to restate the data given in the passage or chart and to switch around variables or symbols.

In this step, you'll probably have to go back to the passage and reread as necessary. Now's the time to figure out what a chart or table really means, to find patterns, and to evaluate the data. Sometimes the question will point you to specific places in the passage or accompanying charts. If not, let the paraphrase of the question you did in Step 2 guide you to the important parts of the passage.

Later in this Intensive we'll describe the one question type for which you can't make a prediction. Not to worry, however: We'll also explain how you can use the answer choices to tackle the question and select the right answer.

Step 4: Match Your Prediction to the Answer Choices. This step is common sense: Pick the choice that best matches your prediction. If you can't find a choice that matches, go back to Steps 2 and 3. Reread the question, check out the passage, and make a new prediction.

THE BIG FOUR QUESTION TYPES

Questions on the ACT Science Test break down as follows: 15 following Data Representation, 18 following Research Summaries, and 7 following Conflicting Viewpoints. Even though the passages differ in content and scope, the 33 questions that follow Data Representation and Research Summaries passages fit into four categories. We've given each type a name that describes what the question wants you to do:

QUESTION TYPE	YOUR TASK
1. Read the Chart	Identify information given in the chart.
2. Use the Chart	Use the information given in the chart to determine other, unstated information.
3. Interpret Graphs	Translate the information in the chart into words or translate words or numbers into a chart.
4. Take the Next Step	Determine what needs to happen next for research experiments to achieve a certain goal.

1. Read the Chart

Read the Chart questions test your ability to locate and understand the information presented in the charts provided in the passage. The answers to these questions are usually explicitly stated within the charts.

Here's an example of a Read the Chart question:

> **6.** According to Table 1, what amount of energy was used to return a spring with a spring constant of 10 to its equilibrium position after it had been displaced by an object with mass M_5 and force 50 N?
>
> **F.** 5 J
> **G.** 25 J
> **H.** 50 J
> **J.** 125 J

This question type is very similar to the Specific Detail questions we covered in the Reading Test Intensive because you're looking for information or data given specifically in the passage. Now let's see how to answer it.

Begin by restating the question. Here, this question asks you about the energy required to bring a certain spring with a certain mass back to equilibrium. Rephrasing the question lets us figure out where to go in the passage: In this case, we'll look at Table 1, specifically Trial 5.

Now that we know which row to look at, we can figure out which column we need and make a prediction. We're looking for the potential energy, or J: M_5 was displaced with a force of 50 N in Trial 5, where 125 J was required to return it to equilibrium. Taking a look at the choices, we see that choice **J** matches our prediction exactly.

Here's another Read the Chart question:

---

1. Which of the following statements about displacement and the force on the spring is consistent with the data in Table 1?

   A. The force on the spring increases as displacement increases.
   B. The force on the spring decreases as displacement increases.
   C. The force on the spring does not change as displacement increases.
   D. The force on the spring increases then decreases as displacement increases.

Restating the question shows us that we need to look at two numbers—the displacement of the spring and the force on the spring—and identify their relationship.

A quick scan of the table shows you that all six trials show displacement increasing (a quick scan of the answer choices tells you the same thing: Each one uses the phrase *displacement increases*). Trials 1–3 and Trials 4–6 both show displacement increasing from 1 meter to 5 meters to 10 meters. We're on our way to making a prediction.

Because we know that displacement increases, we need to check out what happens to the force on the spring. The next step is to check out the corresponding numbers in the Force column. In Trial 1 (a displacement of 1 meter), the force is equal to 5 newtons; in Trial 2 (a displacement of 5 meters), the force is equal to 25 newtons; in Trial 3 (a displacement of 10 meters), the force is equal to 50 newtons. These numbers seem to indicate that force increases with displacement.

Now check whether the statement holds true in Trials 4–6. The force rises from 10 newtons to 50 newtons to 100 newtons; in other words, it increases as displacement increases. You've just successfully formulated an answer to the question ("when displacement increases, force increases"), so you can move on to Step 4 and check out the choices. The correct answer is **A**.

2. Use the Chart

To answer Use the Chart questions, you must use information from the given chart or charts to decipher additional, unstated information (hence the name). For example, some of these questions might ask you to make an informed guess as to what would happen if one of the variables in an experiment changed. This question type is slightly more complicated than Read the Chart questions, because you need to manipulate the info found in the chart.

An example will show you what we mean:

2. According to the information provided in the introduction and Table 1, which of the following is the largest mass?

F. M_1
G. M_3
H. M_5
J. M_6

This question type is very similar to the Inference questions found on the Reading Test because both require you to theorize about or infer something based on what's stated in the passage. Here, the question tells you to refer to both the introduction (the first paragraph, before the visual) and Table 1 to find the largest mass of the four choices. Take a look at the passage in the X-ray again. In the introduction, there are two sentences that will help you answer this question. The first sentence is, *A larger mass will create a larger displacement than a small mass.* This sentence indicates that you should look at the amount of displacement to gauge the relative size of the masses. But if you look only at the displacement, you'd probably wonder how to choose between M_3 and M_6, which both indicate a displacement of 10 meters.

To solve this problem, look to the second crucial sentence in the passage, *The spring constant measures the elasticity of a spring: If a spring has a high k, the spring cannot be stretched easily; if a spring has a low k, it can be stretched more easily.* This sentence points to the difference between the two springs being tested (one with $k = 5$ and the other with $k = 10$). If the spring with $k = 10$ is the tougher to stretch of the two, you can conclude that it requires a heavier mass to stretch the tough spring 10 meters than it does to stretch the weaker spring 10 meters. The heaviest mass is M_6, or **J.**

Let's try another Use the Chart question:

> **3.** If Trial 2 were repeated with a spring with $k = 15$, the displacement of the spring would be:
>
> **A.** less than 5.
> **B.** 5.
> **C.** between 5 and 15.
> **D.** greater than 15.

This question resembles the last one in an important way: Both questions require you understand the sentence, *The spring constant measures the elasticity of a spring: If a spring has a high k, the spring cannot be stretched easily; if a spring has a low k, it can be stretched more easily.*

The sentence about springs tells you that replacing the spring in Trial 2 with a spring that's tougher to pull will result in a smaller displacement of the spring (if the mass pulling on it remains the same). Taking a look at Table 1: When $k = 5$, Trial 2 produces a displacement of 5 meters. So with a larger k ($k = 15$) and the same mass, the displacement must be less than 5 meters. That's **A.**

3. Interpret Graphs

These questions will generally ask you to transform the data given in the charts into graphic form or vice versa. Remember: Straight lines indicate linear functions, while curved lines represent exponential functions. Straight horizontal lines indicate that the variable remains constant. Being able to manipulate and transform data in this way indicates that you have a good grasp of what the given information in the passage means.

For example:

4. Which of the following graphs best represents the change in potential energy with increasing displacement for Trials 1–3?

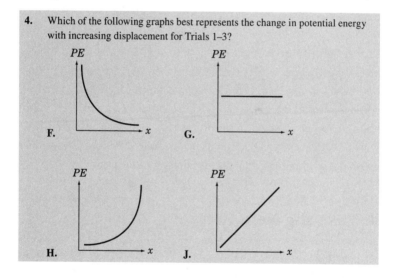

These questions force you to look at the answer choices as you consider the question. You can't make a prediction until you see what you're dealing with. So you need to check out the answer choices and work from there.

Each of the graphs represents displacement on the x-axis, or horizontal axis, while potential energy is represented on the y-axis, or vertical axis. As you move right on the x-axis and up on the y-axis, numerical values increase.

Now that you understand the graphs, you next need to examine the relationship between potential energy and displacement according to Table 1. From the data given in the chart, you can see that potential energy rises as displacement increases. Because you're looking for a rise in potential energy, you can eliminate the first two choices: **F** shows potential energy decreasing with an increase in displacement, and **G** shows potential energy remaining constant. Now you've narrowed down your choices to **H** and **J**.

The key difference between the graphs in these two choices is that **H** shows potential energy rising exponentially and **J** shows it rising linearly. In other words, the potential energy represented in **H** does not increase in direct proportion to displacement; instead, each incremental increase in displacement leads to an ever larger jump in potential energy. From Table 1, you can determine that **H**'s depiction of potential energy is correct because the numbers do not rise in a steady manner (as the numbers for force do).

4. Take the Next Step

Take the Next Step questions present you with a stated goal that can be achieved through experimentation and tests mentioned in the passage. Your job is to choose the answer that would best achieve that goal.

Here's an example:

5. What would be the best method of determining how the spring constant affects displacement?

A. Reproduce Trials 1–6 but use only springs with spring constant $k = 5$.

B. Reproduce Trials 1–3.

C. Reproduce Trials 4–6.

D. Reproduce Trials 1–6 but change the masses in Trials 4–6 to M_1, M_2, and M_3, respectively.

These questions are very similar to the Reading Test's Big Picture questions. Both question types require you to understand the passage as a whole before you can make any predictions about the answer.

Begin by making sure you understand the goal stated in the question. This question wants you to measure how displacement changes when you have different spring constants. The introductory paragraph tells us that large masses create larger displacements than smaller masses.

So in order to figure out how the spring constant affects displacement, we'd want to test the same three masses on the two different spring constants. In other words, we'd want to use M_1, M_2, and M_3 when $k = 5$ and $k = 10$. The correct answer is **D**.

If you got stuck and couldn't make a prediction, you could have evaluated the answer choices to see which one makes sense. You know that the goal calls for testing with different spring constants, so you can eliminate **A**, **B**, and **C** because they all call for the use of just one spring constant. You can double-check that you're right by asking yourself whether **D** makes sense. **D** uses two spring constants ($k = 5$ and $k = 10$), and it proposes that you use the same masses with the second spring that you used with the first. This proposal makes a lot of sense because the only variable will be the spring constant—you won't need to take mass into account in the comparison. So **D** is the correct answer to this problem.

SPECIAL ADVICE FOR CONFLICTING VIEWPOINTS

4

The Conflicting Viewpoints passage presents you with two or three alternative theories on an observable phenomenon and requires you to understand the similarities and differences between the viewpoints. It's really a Reading Test passage in disguise. So your best bet is to review and apply the strategies from the Reading Test Intensive to this passage, including skimming; noting the topic/scope, purpose/main idea, and tone; outlining; and eliminating extreme answers.

Three types of questions follow the Conflicting Viewpoints passage:

- **Detail.** These questions ask you about specific information from the passage. They will address only one viewpoint at a time and usually deal with a key aspect of that viewpoint.
- **Inference.** These questions ask you to make inferences (i.e., figure out the implied information) based on the arguments of each viewpoint. You may also be asked to identify a statement or piece of evidence that lends support to one of the viewpoints.
- **Comparison.** These questions ask you to compare the viewpoints in terms of specific details presented in each argument, to identify points on which the viewpoints would agree or disagree, and to make inferences about the viewpoints.

Recognize them? You should, because these three questions also show up on the Reading Test. Studying for the Reading Test means you're already prepared for answering the questions that follow Conflicting Viewpoints.

PRACTICE SET

Now that you've gotten a handle on the content and format of the Science Test, as well as the strategies to use on test day, it's time for practice.

PASSAGE I

Scientists and doctors have proposed many theories for why the human body begins to break down as it approaches old age. Three of the most common theories are oxidation reaction, suboptimal hormone levels, and cross-linkage.

Oxidation Reaction

5   Oxygen combustion occurs during many biological processes and often results in byproducts called free oxygen radicals. This *singlet oxygen* molecule has only one electron, resulting in a strong electronegative charge that creates a high degree of instability. The molecule generally reacts quickly with any nearby molecules, resulting in the destruction or corruption of cellular parts, including

10   DNA. Free radicals other than singlet oxygen molecules can also be ingested through food, inhaled through air pollutants, or caused by electromagnetic radiation such as X-rays. The cellular damage from free radicals is cumulative; over time, the buildup of damage becomes too great for a cell to continue to function normally.

15   Suboptimal Hormone Levels

The human body relies on a variety of hormones for normal operation. As the body ages, production declines for various glands of hormones such as progesterone, melatonin, androstenedione, testosterone, estrogen, and human growth hormone (HGH). HGH is linked with the general growth and upkeep

20   of cells and organs. Melatonin regulates sleep (a decrease in melatonin levels is associated with difficulty in sleeping) and may help prevent cancer. Testosterone, estrogen, and progesterone together regulate sex drive, bone structure, muscle growth, and mental sharpness. While a slowdown of thyroid hormone production does not always occur, it can cause heart disease. In addition, as the body ages,

25   the production of several hormones, including insulin and cortisol, increases. As insulin levels increase, blood sugar levels respond proportionally. Cortisol is believed to induce stress.

Cross-linkage

Collagen is a protein that plays a major role in the connective tissues of the

30   body. These tissues fill numerous roles, including cushioning and supporting the body. (Cartilage, bone, and tendons are all types of connective tissue.) Collagen can exist in several forms, some soluble, others insoluble. The cross-linkage

theory states that during aging, protein mechanisms called cross-linkages
convert soluble collagen into insoluble collagen. This, in turn, reduces cell
35 elasticity and permeability. The theory holds that cross-linkage reduces passage
of nutrients and waste across cell boundaries and also decreases diffusion of
necessary nutrients to cells far removed from blood capillaries. Cross-linking
agents are prevalent in many types of foods, as well as in environmental factors
such as UV rays in sunlight and highenergy electromagnetic radiation.

1. Which of the following do the cross-linkage and oxidation reaction theories
   agree does NOT cause aging?

   A. Certain protein mechanisms that produce insoluble collagen
   B. Molecular instability in cells
   C. Increased cell elasticity
   D. Detrimental chemical reactions in connective tissues

2. If DNA corruption causes cancer, as many scientists believe, which of the
   theories can help explain cancer as well as aging?

   F. Oxidation reaction
   G. Suboptimal hormone levels
   H. Cross-linkage
   J. None of the theories can adequately explain the cause of cancer.

3. Elastin is a protein in the skin that can become less effective or even harmful due
   to excess solar radiation. A likely agent of elastin's decay is:

   A. low levels of insulin.
   B. cross-linkage agents.
   C. connective tissues.
   D. high stress levels.

4. Scientists in a medical laboratory find that mice kept in an iron-covered
   environment age at slightly slower rate than mice that are not. Which of the
   following explanations, if true, would support both the oxidation reaction theory
   and the cross-linkage theory?

   F. Iron helps deflect electromagnetic radiation.
   G. Iron particles in the air enter the mice as antioxidants.
   H. Iron particles in the bloodstream tend to make proteins soluble.
   J. Iron particles aid in the production of HGH.

5. Which of the following is an argument in favor of oxidation reaction over suboptimal hormone levels to explain the overall cause of aging?

A. Free radicals can exert cellular damage on glands.
B. Children with unusually low levels of HGH seem to age faster.
C. As life expectancy in many countries has increased, so has pollution.
D. Obesity often leads to premature cellular stress and damage.

6. A pharmaceutical company develops a drug that enhances the ability of cells to rebuild structures that have sustained long-term damage.According to which theory would this drug be the most effective at slowing the aging process?

F. Oxidation reaction
G. Suboptimal hormone levels
H. Cross-linkage
J. None of the theories would predict this drug to help against aging.

7. Doctors at a certain hospital begin to notice that a number of older patients had tissues damaged by excess blood sugar content. According to the suboptimal hormone levels theory, which of the following is the most likely explanation?

A. The thyroid gland has become overactive.
B. Insulin production has increased.
C. Progesterone levels have dropped.
D. Melatonin levels have risen to higher-than-normal levels.

PASSAGE II

Baseball players use a bat to hit a thrown ball. Generally, hitters want to use a bat that will hit a ball as far as possible. Since the start of the sport, bat manufacturers have experimented with different shapes, designs, and types of wood in order to produce optimal bats. One important principle of bat design is
5 the "sweet spot"—a location on the barrel of the bat that produces the greatest distance for a hit ball. (Batters often note that a ball hit on the sweet spot will produce almost no resistance at all, whereas a ball hit on another part of the bat can produce jarring, painful vibrations.) The sweet spot is roughly halfway between the endpoint of the barrel and the point where the barrel narrows to the
10 handle (in Figure 1, the narrow handle is on the right and the barrel is on the left).

Figure 1

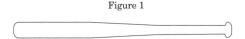

The force that a batter applies to a bat when he or she swings can be roughly modeled by the following equations:

$$F = ma$$
$$a = \frac{v}{t}$$

F is the total force applied to the bat by the hitter, m is the mass (equivalent in this case to weight) of the bat, a is the rotational acceleration of the bat, v is the
15 velocity of the middle of the bat, and t is the time of the swing. Assuming a batter is swinging as hard as possible, the amount of force exerted is constant from swing to swing.

Table 1 shows tests done with a machine to test several bat models at constant swing velocities. Note that maple is a harder wood than ash.

Table 1

Wood Type	Length (inches)	Weight (ounces)	Travel distance (feet)
Ash	34	28	406
Ash	34	30	412
Ash	34	32	418
Ash	36	30	412
Ash	36	32	418
Maple	34	28	414
Maple	34	30	428
Maple	34	32	440
Maple	36	30	428
Maple	36	32	440

8. When a ball hits the sweet spot, it will travel:

F. a greater distance than if it hits any other part of the bat.
G. a shorter distance than if it hits any other part of the bat.
H. the same distance as if it hits any other part of the bat.
J. no distance at all.

9. Which of the following illustrates the relationship between velocity of the bat and the distance a hit ball will travel?

 A.

 B.

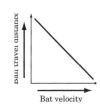

C.

J.

10. Which of the following statements is true, according to the data in the passage and Table 1?

F. The weight of a bat has more effect than the length of the bat on the distance a ball will travel.

G. A bat swung with greater speed than another will not make a ball travel farther, assuming all other factors are constant.

H. A 36-inch bat is generally better than a 34-inch bat.

J. A shorter maple bat is more effective than a longer maple bat.

11. Which of the following would most likely not make a ball travel farther?

A. Using a metal bat, which is harder than either wood

B. The batter adopting a "tighter" batting swing, meaning the arc of the bat through the swing will be smaller

C. Using a bat made from a heavier type of wood than either ash or maple

D. The batter lifting weights to increase arm strength and bat velocity

12. Based on the passage, which of the following historical baseball developments would be expected to result in baseballs being hit farther?

F. Batters using tar pine to get a better grip on the bat handle

G. Baseballs wound tighter (made harder)

H. New baseball parks made smaller than old ones

J. Batters using gloves to reduce the sting on the hands from a badly hit ball

13. In the 1950s, professional baseball players began using bats that had thinner handles, although the barrel ends of the bats stayed about the same width. (In fact, the bat in Figure 1 is one of these "modern" bats.) What might the advantage be of such a bat?

A. The newer bat would have greater durability.

B. The newer bat could be swung faster.

C. The newer bat would have a larger sweet spot.

D. The newer bat would be longer.

PASSAGE III

The liquid phase of any substance consists of molecules moving with varying amounts of kinetic energy. Additionally, each substance has a distinct, invariant molecular force that pulls molecules of that liquid together. When a molecule's kinetic energy exceeds the bonding forces in the liquid, it escapes from the

5 liquid's surface and exists in gaseous form. If kept in a closed container, these molecules will exert pressure on the container. This pressure is called *vapor pressure*. Also, note that any liquid will boil (turn completely to gas) when the vapor pressure reaches 760 mm Hg.

Table 1 shows the vapor pressures of different liquids at different

10 temperatures. Vapor pressure is measured in mm Hg.

Table 1

Temperature	Water	Ethyl alcohol	Benzene	Carbon tetrachloride
−15°C	1.62	4.55	11.23	13.57
0°C	4.58	12.17	27.51	33.34
15°C	12.72	32.22	57.97	71.08
30°C	31.83	78.76	118.16	142.56
45°C	71.91	174.04	225.31	263.42
60°C	149.38	352.69	389.52	450.93
75°C	289.09	666.13	642.89	720.18

Figure 1 shows vapor pressure versus temperature for the same liquids.

Figure 1

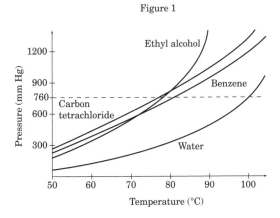

14. Which liquid's vapor pressure increases least as its temperature increases from 0 to 60° C?

    F. Water
    G. Ethyl alcohol
    H. Benzene
    J. Carbon tetrachloride

15. Which of the following best illustrates the relationship between molecular bond strength and vapor pressure?

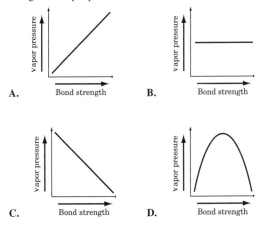

16. Compared to benzene, the molecular bonds in water are:

    F. stronger.

    G. weaker.

    H. about the same.

    J. impossible to compare.

17. Which liquid will boil at the lowest temperature?

    A. Water

    B. Benzene

    C. Carbon tetrachloride

    D. Ethyl alcohol

18. Which experiment would best help to determine whether the force of attraction between molecules varies as a substance changes phase?

    F. Measuring the vapor pressure of a frozen mixture of the four substances in the chart

    G. Freezing ice to extremely low temperatures (below) and measuring vapor pressure

    H. Comparing the vapor pressures of ice, liquid benzene, and gaseous ethyl alcohol

    J. Comparing the vapor pressures of ice and water at its melting point, and comparing the vapor pressures of solid and liquid benzene at its melting point

Guided Explanations

1. C

Passage I is a Conflicting Viewpoints passage. Don't worry too much if you were stumped or confused by any of the questions: You'll see just one of these types of passages on test day.

We'll assume that you skimmed and outlined the passage first. This Detail question wants you to compare two theories and figure out which of the answers is not listed as a cause of aging in the first and the last theories listed in the passage. **A** is incorrect because the cross-linkage theory states that one of the reasons for aging is the protein mechanisms that convert soluble collagen to insoluble collagen. **B** is incorrect because the oxidation reaction theory states that free radicals are unstable molecules that are attracted to other molecules and lead to cellular damage. **C** is correct because neither of the two theories holds that increased cell elasticity causes aging. The cross-linkage theory actually states that a reduction in cell elasticity contributes to aging, while the oxidation reaction theory is silent on the matter. **D** is incorrect because the cross-linkage theory states that connective tissue is where collagen becomes insoluble.

2. F

To answer this Inference question, you need to see which theory could account for DNA corruption. **F** is correct because the passage states that free radicals can disrupt DNA molecules, which in turn can lead to cancer. **G** is incorrect because none of the hormones listed have an effect on DNA. **H** is incorrect because the cross-linkage that makes collagen insoluble is not said to have an effect on DNA. **J** is incorrect because one of the theories (oxidation reaction) does offer an explanation as to the cause of cancer.

3. B

Two details in this Inference question are especially important: the facts that elastin is a protein and that it can be damaged by the radiation in sunlight. This suggests a process similar to the cross-linkage of collagen. **A** is incorrect because an excess of insulin leads to increased blood sugar but does not necessarily affect proteins. **B** is correct because cross-linkage agents are said to be responsible for the conversion of soluble collagen to harmful insoluble collagen, and can be found in sunlight. **C** is incorrect because connective tissues themselves have no effect on elastin. **D** is incorrect because high stress levels are an effect of excess levels of cortisol, which is unrelated to elastin.

4. F

Each potential answer to this Comparison question needs to be examined to see whether it is in accordance with the oxidation reaction theory and the cross-linkage theory. **F** is correct because both theories state that electromagnetic radiation can be the cause of aging (free radicals in the oxidation reaction and cross-linkage agents in the cross-linkage theory). **G** is incorrect because only the oxidation reaction theory states that free radicals cause aging. **H** is incorrect because increased protein solubility would support only the cross-linkage theory. **J** is incorrect because neither of the two theories states that HGH (human growth hormone) slows the aging process.

5. A

To answer this Comparison question, you need to find the answer that best promotes the oxidation reaction theory over the suboptimal hormone levels theory. **A** is correct because the suboptimal hormone levels theory states that hormone production declines during aging but does not directly describe why the glands that produce the hormones decay. The oxidation reaction theory suggests a way in which this might occur. **B** is incorrect because it is in favor of the hormone levels theory. **C** is incorrect because it is an argument against the oxidation reaction theory (pollution causes free radicals, which contribute to aging in the oxidation reaction theory). **D** is incorrect because neither theory explicitly mentions obesity as a cause of aging.

6. F

The answer to this Comparison question is the theory in which general cellular damage is the most direct cause of aging. **F** is correct because in the oxidation reaction theory cellular damage occurs cumulatively, which leads to aging when cells can no longer rebuild themselves. **G** is incorrect because the primary cause of aging in the suboptimal hormone levels theory is incorrect glandular production of hormones, and it is less clear that faster cellular rebuilding would have as great an effect against aging. **H** is incorrect because the cross-linkage theory states conversion of collagen, a protein, into insoluble form is the cause of aging, so increased cellular rebuilding would not be as effective against aging. **J** is incorrect because the oxidation reaction theory predicts this drug would be extremely helpful against aging.

7. B

The set concludes with a Detail question. The hormone level theory states that insulin level increases lead to blood sugar increases. **A** is incorrect because an under-productive thyroid can lead to heart disease, so an over-productive thyroid is unlikely to lead to high blood sugar levels. **B** is correct because insulin is mentioned as being related to blood sugar levels. **C** is incorrect because progesterone helps regulate muscle growth and bone maintenance, among other things, but does not have a direct effect on blood sugar. **D** is incorrect because melatonin regulates sleep, not blood sugar.

8. F

This Research Summaries passage implies that the sweet spot is the area of the bat where the maximum energy is transferred from bat to ball, making the flight of the ball as long as possible. Thus **F** is correct, and **G**, **H**, and **J** are incorrect.

9. C

This is an Interpret Graphs question. In the first equation, you can substitute v/t for a in order to get a better idea of how velocity affects the force exerted by the bat. Making this substitution gives $F = mv/t$. This new equation means that as bat velocity increases, the force increases in a linear manner, as does the distance the ball travels. **A** is incorrect because it shows distance increasing exponentially as velocity increases. **D** is incorrect because it shows distance decreasing as velocity increases. **C** is correct because it shows distance increasing linearly along with velocity. **B**, like **D**, is incorrect because it shows distance decreasing as velocity increases.

10. F

To answer this Use the Chart question, you need to look carefully at all the answers to see which one is consistent with the passage. **F** is correct because the chart shows that for the same wood and same weight, the length of the bat has no effect on distance, whereas for the same wood and same length, the weight of the bat will affect distance. **G** is incorrect because the equation shows that a bat swung with greater velocity will have greater force to impart to the ball, driving it farther. **H** is incorrect because the passage shows no difference between the lengths traveled by balls hit by bats of different lengths. **J** is incorrect because the table shows that maple bats of two different lengths do equally well, if other conditions are identical.

11. B

Another Use the Chart question. **A** is incorrect because metal is harder than wood, so a metal bat would presumably hit a ball farther. **B** is correct because there is nothing in the passage that suggests that a smaller swing would lead to greater power. **C** is incorrect because Table 1 states that the heavier bats are more effective. **D** is incorrect because greater arm strength would presumably enable the batter to exert more force on the bat.

12. G

To get this Take the Next Step question correct, you need to find the answer that, together with the information in the passage, would lead to baseballs traveling farther. **F** is incorrect because there is no mention of grip in the passage (nor is it measured in any equations). **G** is correct because the passage states that maple is harder than ash. The maple bats make the ball travel farther, which suggests that a harder ball might travel farther than a softer one. **H** is incorrect—it might result in more home runs, but it has no effect on the distance hit balls travel. **J** is incorrect because there is no mention of hands in the passage and they are not accounted for in the data.

13. B

Another Take the Next Step question. Recall the force equation: $F = ma$. Assuming that the force exerted by the batter on the bat (the value on the left) remains constant, and the mass of the bat decreases (due to the thinner handle), the acceleration (a) will increase, resulting in greater bat velocity. This, in turn, makes the ball travel farther. **A** is incorrect because there is no reason to think that a thinner bat would be more durable (it turns out that modern bats are a lot more likely to break). **B** is correct because newer bats could be swung faster. **C** is incorrect because the barrel size remains the same, so there is nothing that suggests the sweet spot would become larger (in fact, it gets smaller). **D** is incorrect because making the handle thinner is unrelated to the length of the bat.

14. F

Passage III is a Data Representations passage. As always, begin by skimming and outlining the passage. Don't forget to pay attention to the details and to take notes. To answer this Read the Chart question, you need only look at Table 1 (Figure 1 doesn't begin until 50°). **F** is correct because the vapor pressure of water increases 144.8 mm Hg, whereas the vapor pressures of the other liquids increase by more than 300 mm Hg.

15. C

To answer this Interpret Graphs question, it's key to realize that when molecular bond strength increases, it becomes less likely for a molecule to have the amount of kinetic energy necessary to overcome these bonds. As bond strength increases, vapor pressure decreases because vapor pressure is a measure of the relative number of molecules with sufficient kinetic energy to become vaporous. **A** is incorrect because it shows vapor pressure increasing with bond strength. **B** is incorrect because it shows vapor pressure being unaffected by bond strength. **C** is correct because it shows vapor pressure decreasing as bond strength increases. **D** is incorrect because it shows vapor pressure increasing, then decreasing as bond strength increases.

16. F

This is a Use the Chart question. The stronger the molecular bonds, the less likely it is that an individual molecule will have sufficient kinetic energy to break free and become vapor. **F** is correct because water has a lower vapor pressure than benzene at comparable temperatures, which means its bonds are stronger. **G** is incorrect because water would have a higher vapor pressure than benzene if its bonds were weaker. **H** is incorrect because water and benzene do not have the same vapor pressures. **J** is incorrect because the data in the table allows you to determine the relative strength of the bonds.

17. C

Another Use the Chart question. Remember that any liquid will boil when its vapor pressure reaches 760 mm Hg. To find the answer, you need to look at Figure 1 and find the line that crosses 760 mm Hg the farthest to the left (at the lowest temperature). **A**, **B**, and **D** are incorrect because they are farther to the right than carbon tetrachloride. **C** is correct because the line for carbon tetrachloride crosses the 760 mm Hg line farthest to the left.

18. J

To answer this Take the Next Step question, you need to look for the experiment that will most closely look at the effect of phase change on vapor pressure for individual substances. **F** is incorrect because measuring the vapor pressure of a frozen mixture would not be very useful in gaining information about individual substances. **G** is incorrect because we are interested in phase changes, and ice at various temperatures is still in the same phase. **H** is incorrect because it involves comparisons of different phases, but for different substances (comparing ice to liquid benzene, for instance, says nothing about the effects of phase changes on water's vapor pressure). **J** is correct because it isolates the experiment for phase changes of an individual substance rather than for temperature and does this for two different substances separately.

Top 15 ACT Test-Day Tips

HERE ARE OUR 15 TIPS FOR DOING YOUR BEST ON TEST DAY:

'Twas the Night Before the ACT . . .

#15: Get it together. Pack up the day before so you don't have to go scrambling around in the morning. If you're bringing a calculator to use on the Math Test, make sure it has batteries. Get your admission ticket, ID, water, and nonsugar energy snack (for the break) all ready to go.

#14: Wind down. Runners don't run a full marathon the day *before*; they rest up for the big day. Avoid cramming the day before the test. Read a book, watch a movie, hang out with friends, whatever relaxes you—but make it an early night. And speaking of which . . .

#13: Get enough sleep. Don't get into bed at 7:00 just to stare at the ceiling, but do get to bed early enough to ensure you have enough sleep to be alert and energetic for test day.

#12: Set two alarms. You don't want to miss the test because your alarm was set for PM instead of AM—stranger things have happened. Also, one of your alarms should be battery-operated, just in case something crazy like a power outage occurs during the night. Unlikely, sure, but peace of mind will help you sleep better.

Rise and Shine . . .

#11: Eat normally. Sure, test day is special, but that doesn't mean you need to treat yourself to a special breakfast. Nerves can turn a huge bacon, egg, and cheese omelet against you—especially if you don't usually eat that kind of thing. Eat what you normally eat for breakfast—not too much, not too little. Bring a nonsugar snack for the break. It's a long day, and you'll need the energy.

#10: Dress for success. One word: *layers*. If it's hot, take some off. If it's cold, leave them on. Comfort is key.

#9: Jump-start your brain. To employ the marathon analogy again (see #14), runners stretch before the big event to warm up. Likewise, it helps to do a bit of reading before the test to get your mind warmed up and stretch those brain cells into shape. We're not talking Plato or Shakespeare here. Articles from a well-written newspaper, magazine, or journal containing the same kind of writing you'll see on the test will do.

Put on Your Game Face . . .

#8: Arrive early. Save fashionable lateness for your social life. Rushing around like a crazy person isn't the best way to start test day. If the testing center is in unfamiliar territory, you may even wish to scout it out ahead of time just to be sure you know your way. One less thing to worry about couldn't hurt.

#7: Don't sweat the small stuff. Okay, so what if it's 9 billion degrees in the testing room and that obnoxious kid from chem class is right next to you? If something potentially correctable is bothering you, by all means talk to a proctor, but if there's nothing you can do about it, *let it go.* Don't allow small annoyances to distract you from your mission.

#6: Gear up for a long haul. Some people arrive at the test center all revved up, bouncing off the walls—*the big day is finally here!* Slow down; you don't want to overheat and peak too soon. You'll get to the test site, endure the usual standardized testing bureaucratic technicalities, and probably fill out a bunch of paperwork. "Go time" isn't until the proctor tells you to open the test booklet. Which brings us to our tips for the final and most important phase of the testing experience . . .

Go Time . . .

#5: Know what to expect. The ACT Subject Tests are always given in the following order: English, Math, Reading, Science, and Writing (which is optional). You need to be ready to start the test by answering questions about passages of absolutely no interest to you, followed by questions about tricky figures and equations.

#4: Keep your focus. Maybe the girl to the right of you will appear to breeze through the first section in five minutes, while the guy to the left of you seems unaware that a test is even taking place. If you have a large enough group, chances are someone may even freak out and leave the room in tears. Assuming that this person isn't you, don't let it bother you. Stay focused on your objective and let the others take care of themselves.

#3: Choose your battles. No one question can hurt you significantly unless you spend all day on it. Keep moving through each section. If a question isn't working for you, guess and move on.

#2: **Stick it out.** There may come a time in the last section when you'll do anything to end your agony five minutes early. Hang in there and keep applying what you've learned. True champs finish strong.

And the #1 Test Day Tip . . . Relax. Nerves are normal, but how you deal with them is up to you. Channel your adrenaline positively to give you the energy you need to maintain your focus all the way through. Also remember that while the test is surely important, *it's not the most important thing in the world*. Put the event into perspective. Then do the best you can, which is the most you can ask of yourself.

FINAL THOUGHT

Sure, maybe you could have started prepping sooner, but it's too late for that now. Banish the "coulda, woulda, shoulda" thoughts from your head and focus on the task at hand: doing your best on test day.

We at SparkNotes wish you the best of luck!

SPARK COLLEGE

www.sparkcollege.com

FIND YOUR BEST FIT

Finding the right college or university can be scary, but SparkCollege has made it easy!

Take a simple and fun personality test to find the right type of school for you.

Search through our database to keep tabs on schools you'd like to visit, apply to, or ever reach for.

Get help with applying to, paying for, and even surviving your first year!

It's all here, just for you.

www.sparkcollege.com